THREE STEPS TO GOD

GLEN L. BOLLINGER

THREE STEPS TO GOD

By Glen L. Bollinger

ISBN: 979-8-9894450-0-4

Book Cover & Interior Design by Exodus Design Studio
www.ExodusDesign.com

Printed in the United States of America

Acknowledgments

I would like to dedicate this book to my mama and daddy. They both loved me unconditionally and never really showed anger towards me, even though I often deserved it. My daddy always tried to guide me in the right direction and he always wanted the best for me. My mama always kept that book, the Bible, nearby and read it daily—a book I have come to love myself. They both prayed for me as I took many steps in the wrong direction early in my life. God honored those prayers and brought me to Him in an everlasting love. I will be forever grateful for having them as my earthly parents, and look forward to seeing them again one day in Heaven!

Number one, I thank God for saving me and giving me this story to write some 14 years ago, helping me to complete it, and all honor goes to Him.

I thank my wife Cynde, for sticking with me through the thick and thin of our marriage, being my best friend and giving me encouragement along the way through the process of getting this book done and everything else!

I want to thank our two children, Jack Garner and Keziah, for helping me with this project and also giving me encouragement when I needed it. They are both wonderful children and have such great purpose ahead for their lives. I am proud of them both!

I want to thank my big brother Darryl, as an accomplished author in his own right or is that write? Oh well, anyway, he has helped me tremendously, giving me encouragement and advice throughout the whole process. I couldn't have done it without him.

I want to thank Dr. Jim for not only helping me through a very difficult time in my personal life, but also for encouraging me to finish what God gave me to do in the writing of this book.

And finally, I want to thank my friends and family for their help and encouragement, many of them having stuck with me for a good bit of time, and some of them for only a short while, regardless of my faults. They are not listed in order of priority for they all mean so much to me: Pat and Mort, Judy and Lamar, Marlene and Mike, Wayne, Liz, Charles, and Bob.

I would also like to thank my editor, Eddy Oliver with Hopscotch Creative, LLC, for all of his help in making this book a realty and no longer just a dream.

And finally, I would like to thank Kristine and staff with Exodus Design Studio for helping me with the graphics and all the other details to get my book to the readers.

TABLE OF CONTENTS

INTRODUCTION

My hope and desire for this book is that it will appeal to at least two main "wide groups" of thinkers. The number one group would be the people who consider themselves skeptics or people who don't really believe in God as being true. It doesn't matter at this point why you have your idea or opinion about this. What matters is, are you willing to at least consider and put away for a little bit your preconceived notions on this subject? In other words, are you willing to open your being and yourself to at least ponder and think of the things that will be brought out in this step-by-step process? Ask yourself "what is it here in front of me, is there truth, and is there something to this that I need to really take a look at?" If you are in this first group of people and you are able to answer these last questions with an affirmative, then you've already begun the process.

The second group of people would be those who already believe that God is true and have accepted this as such. Many in this group may have trusted in Christ as their Savior at some point in their life and they call themselves "Christian." This book hopefully will help give you some ideas and some information in order to help you "defend," not argue, why you believe what you believe. Some of us just grew up and took what people told us as truth and that's how we live our lives. It's just what we're told, but there's a lot more to it and I think that as Christians we lack in being able to tell others why we believe what we do. It is important to give reasons why you believe the books of the Bible and what it's all about. I think we should all be better at giving testimony to others and we've fallen so short in that ability as Christians.

So, you may not necessarily fit into either of these two groups of people. You haven't ever put a lot of thought into it or maybe you are somewhere in the middle. Regardless of where you would place yourself in this thinking, this book could help your walk in life.

Most things in life are taken in steps. As an infant we crawl around and at some point, we take that first step. That could be the first in the thousands upon thousands of steps we take throughout our life. Usually before a home is constructed, there are plans drawn up detailing all the different parts of the process. There are items such as the grading of dirt, foundation, walls, roof, interior, wiring, plumbing, etc. After the plans are developed, each part has to be completed in a specific order. Failure to follow the plan may result in many problems and some parts cannot even be started until the preceding "piece of the puzzle" is in place. We learn in steps, building on fundamental truths to establish the foundation. Then, we move on as we gain more and more knowledge to understand each additional piece of the total concept or subject. This is how it works as we start out learning the basics. We progress and build upon our learning until we reach the point of having mastered the subject, at least to a point. We really never quit learning most things because usually there's always more to learn.

Steps are taken in everything--when you take a shower, when you prepare a meal, when you go to the grocery store, when you clean your house and when you go on a trip. Just about anything you do requires steps to get there unless it's just one big step and you're there. Our neighbor makes some of the best brownies I have ever eaten; they are so good and so tasty. I don't know what they are, but I'm sure that Marlene takes steps in baking these tasty treats. My wife makes homemade cinnamon rolls and it takes a while because she uses a yeast-type dough. It has to be prepared and then you have to wait until it rises. She then prepares the icing, the nuts (oh yeah, pecans) and all the other things that go into these creations. When they come out of the oven and she puts the icing on the buns, there is nothing on the planet in the form of dessert that tastes better! Thankfully, she only makes them occasionally…. OKAY rarely.

I had a project outside of our home not long after it was constructed. It involved pouring concrete steps to go from the main level outside around to the front of the basement area. My neighbor and friend, Mike, helped me with this project and guess what? It took us steps to make steps! I'm not kidding. We had to dig it out and prepare the ground. We had to build concrete forms and mix the concrete. We had to place stones inside the concrete and then finally, we had to remove the forms. The point here is that it was a process and it all involved steps.

I want to apply all of this step-taking as we look at the questions of God. Is there a God? How do we know? What evidence is there? What has happened in the past? What do we do with what we have around us and what can we learn about it? Going forward, what does the future hold? All of these are valid questions that most folks probably, at one time or another, ask. About fourteen years ago I was given the thought about taking these questions and providing answers in a "three main steps" process.

We can take a look at steps toward God in this simple outline. The first step we will cover and try to answer is what evidence do we have that indicates there is a God and what supports that. How do we know what we have as written in the Bible true and given by God to us? How did it get to us in order to know more about Him and how did it all come about? The first part of this book will lay the foundational answers for these questions.

The second step, as we build on the first, we will take is looking at what we have as written letters from God, also known as "the Bible." This will be to provide or open some understanding of the individual books as a very short description of some of the contents of each book. This second part will briefly describe some of the stories told in these books.

The third and final step, as we build on the first and second one, will try to tie everything together in order to hopefully better understand this amazing story. In this final step, I will try to explain some of how God operated in the past and what He offers today for everyone in the world. The information provided will include revelation of how He offers to reestablish that fellowship with Him and what this story means to us as humans.

I personally believe that there has to be order and truth to God. It's up to us to seek and discover what the story of it all is. It's a beautiful mystery of the things offered to us by a loving Creator. We can all have it if we just trust and accept the gift. So, another way of comparing the method of step-taking in this book is to the game of baseball. You go to first base, then to second, then to third, then to home plate…you take steps to get there.

One of the main things I would ask of anyone who reads this book is that you keep your mind and heart open as you consider what is written. At least for the period of time it takes you to read this, put aside your preconceived notions or even what you may have been taught and accepted as truth about the existence of God. Come with me, let's take a few steps!

"Providence does its work gradually, and by steps."
Matthew Henry

PART ONE:
THE FIRST STEP -
THE BOOK OF BOOKS

WHERE IT ALL CAME FROM
AND HOW WE GOT IT

*"Never let the sense of past failure
defeat your next step."*[1]

CHAPTER ONE
A STARTING POINT

I encourage you, as I often tell folks, to check out for yourself what I say, make sure it lines up as truth and is not just my opinion. There are many resources available, in fact, more than at any other time in history that can be studied. Now along with these good resources, there are some that are not so good as well. So, you have to be careful of your sources as you study and seek the truth. After all, that is how I have lived my life, not necessarily taking someone's word about something. I have to find out for myself. Everything in this book can be verified including the personal work that God can do in a person's life. Just ask around; there are thousands upon thousands of examples.

I believe it's important for us to look at where it all came from and how we got it. For the purposes of this book, I do not want anyone to think I am trying to imitate a scholar. To be clear, I am not. The details surrounding the evidence such as the history of the writings are not only my observations. These can be very verified or confirmed through the many reliable academic resources available. In other words, the focus of this book is not so much digging into every little detail surrounding the dates and the times of discovery. I only wish to give an overall picture of the validity of these findings.

I suppose that as long as people have been around, they have wondered where did they come from, where did the world come from, and where did all the stars and planets come from? What is all this about and what is the reason for it all? Speaking for myself, I have to be counted among those that have wondered. You can just take a night and look at the stars. It's kind of overwhelming to see how small we are and how far off those objects are in the distance. Can we be alone? How did it all get there in the first place? I believe these questions are built into us as humans and part of what makes us different than all the other animals that are here on earth. Can you imagine a dog or a cat just pondering, where am I? What is this place I am in? Who are these creatures that feed and take care of me? Where do I fit in with the scheme of things? Maybe they do, but I kind of doubt it. As long as they have food, water and companionship they seem to be happy. Not a lot of thinking about the questions of life itself and the point of what happens when they die. Again, I believe these questions are built into humans as though there is something missing within us until we find the answers.

There are plenty of theories and ideas on our place here in the universe and no doubt a good many religions have been conceived to go along with them. I am a Christian and believe that I have found the answers to some of these questions. I have not found all of the answers, but the most important ones relating to myself and my soul's destiny, I believe I have. I think this is very important (to me, the most important) to all of us and believe that directions were given so we could live a life with meaning and purpose. Then, after this physical life in our body here on earth, our spiritual soul will continue to live for eternity somewhere.

This is the first step in our journey as we look into the evidence that can be tested, tried and examined. We can then come to conclusions by way of the facts. Yes, I said facts because that's what they are, not theories, not just beliefs. I hope the overwhelming amount of factual evidence that we have will help convince you of this reality. I realize much of what we believe is what we have been taught, not necessarily what we have looked into and examined for ourselves. I grew up asking "why" a lot and my dad would say "son you ask a lot of questions" and I could tell he grew weary of providing answers. I still ask a lot of questions. I encourage you to look into the things brought out in this writing and seek for yourself the truth. The truth will set you free.

So, when people start looking at where they buy a car or where they buy a new washer and dryer, sometimes they really do their homework. They take steps. I have a friend who will spend months researching and getting all the facts on a new appliance before he makes the purchase. All of this makes me wonder why people aren't willing to do the same research on eternity. There are all sorts of options out there and all kind of flavors of religions. What I say to people is, check them out, do some research and look into where their so-called truth came from and then make your mind up. If you look at the Bible strictly from a practical point, you will find the evidence for reliability and accuracy unmatched to anything on the planet.

These ideas came after a discussion with my father-in-law

and his statement that "there are many religions to choose from." This is true. He went on to say that "regardless of what people choose it doesn't matter because they can believe whatever they want to believe. So, you can believe one, all, or none." I wanted to be able to provide an answer to him on the points he made. My contention is that we all have a choice, but it is a choice we have to make. I say, do your homework.

I am not trying to convince you, as a car or insurance salesman may try to do, of your need for these items. I am only a fellow human being attempting to explain, again not convincing, some of the basic simple truths that I understand. This "step method" will provide a path forward to help you understand some of the answers to what many people search for in their lives. I'd also like to mention is that I am not trying to convince you to join some particular denomination or church group. It is important for us to find people who you can fellowship with on this journey and if you don't have that fellowship already, I would encourage you to find it. As people, we are designed to interact with other people and not live an isolated life.

A man's heart plans his way,
But the Lord directs his steps.
- Proverbs 16:9

Chapter Two
It's All In The Text

The evidence of writings about God are contained within a book we call the Bible. As we take our first step and investigate what we have as answers, we need to look at what we already have in writing or text. Where did what we have come from; how did it originate; how did it get to us? Who is this God and how do we know what we have is true? The documents I will be referring to are also known as a collection of books that are contained within one book: the Bible.

The Bible is divided up into two main parts, the Old Testament and the New Testament. The Old Testament books are what came from a period of time written before the birth of Jesus Christ. And the New Testament books are what came from a period of time after the birth of Christ. The total span of time in which these books were written was around 2,000 years. It was put together by at least forty 40 different authors and it contains various letters, poems, songs, and other writings.

For the purpose of this book, I do not wish to explain or argue over the many different interpretations people have on certain parts of the Bible. I would like to give insight to the main tenets contained within it. I personally believe that some of the confusion and misunderstanding of the word of God are brought on by humans. We sometimes get the idea that we can understand these writings in our own human method. In other words, if we can't completely understand the why and when of things revealed in this book, we want to change them or throw them out. If you start out with the idea that this came from God, that should indicate that we do not have the capacity to understand everything about how it came about. We don't have the mind of God. Instead, what we tend to do is figure out all these things in our own way and it helps us to make it fit for us as we see it. Again, that is not the purpose of this book, and please keep this in mind while you read the pages that follow.

So how do we know there is a God? How did this God come about? Where is He and many other questions? I am not going to suggest I can give you an answer to every question you may have and that is not the purpose of this book. As human beings we all reason things out and look at the logical, "how to, what if, how did that happen" kind of thinking and it comes natural for us to do so. I would like to first establish the fact that the book we hold as "letters from God" is the Bible. This enables us to understand how it can be accepted as reliable and true. This can be accomplished by looking at the way it came to us and the way it has been preserved for generations. Of course, God can be found in many things around us. Just look at a sunrise or check out the design of some of the animals on this planet. More specifically, look at humans and at how complex of a being we really are. Take a look at the way the earth is positioned among the other planets and stars. Look at where the moon "just happens to be." If you just take a minute, you will soon find that everything is precisely placed where it all works out for us. Not too close, not too far, but just in the right place. Let's just take away all those examples and look at some of the written or recorded words for a few moments. We will look at the evidence toward God as we take that first step. Come along.

"Don't be so skeptical" I remember saying as a vacuum cleaner salesman back in my early twenties. That's what we would say to folks that opened the door and we proclaimed, "I would like to give you a set of steak knives or a six-pack of soft drinks. And I mean give it to you. You don't have to buy anything, you just let me come in and show you a vacuum cleaner. The gift will be absolutely free and yours to keep." So, I ask you, the reader, to not start out skeptical, but to allow me to show you these steps. That's all... you don't have to buy anything and you're under no obligation. I just ask that you first open your mind to taking these three steps, one step at a time. Don't go into this thinking about all the reasoning you may already have in life to discount the possibilities of the truth in these critical steps. I realize much of what we believe in life is what we have been taught, not necessarily what we looked into and examined for ourselves. As I said earlier, I grew up asking "why" and my dad would say, "son you ask a lot of questions." I encourage you to look into the things brought out in this book for yourself. Don't be afraid to dig into the details and seek to verify and validate what the truth is.

In my walk in life, as far back as I can remember anyway, there was always a familiar book around the house. For that matter, most of the folks in my related family, aunts and uncles and such, you would always see this book nearby. That book was the Bible and the location depended on which house I was in at the time. You know, located on the coffee table, end table, or on a shelf of the bookcase. Many times it would also be placed nearby in the bedrooms on a table with a lamp for nighttime reading. I never really thought much about this book in those days; it was just part of who most of our relatives were. It was always nearby. This book, I have since discovered, has a history much further back than my family or for that matter, anyone that has been on this planet we call earth. The Bible is a book unlike any other which has been written in many ways. I will go into more detail in the following chapters.

For the purposes of this book, I would like to again state that I do not wish to make arguments of such things that many people find pleasure in doing. For instance, is the day mentioned in Genesis really a literal day or is it perhaps thousands of years long? Or where do dinosaurs fit into this creation mixture? Or the very ideas of the evolution theory itself. I believe that if you begin your walk with God and continue with it, He will work all of these ideas out and you will be able at some point to settle these things in your heart one way or the other.

I will attempt to share what we have in the way of written evidence for our Maker and what we have in the way of writings. The main book that Christianity is based on is the Bible. It is now divided up into what is made up of 39 referred to as the Old Testament. It was originally written in the Hebrew language along with a few chapters written in Aramaic before the birth of Jesus Christ. There are 27 books in the New Testament, which was originally written in Greek after the life of Jesus Christ.

Furthermore, the Bible was not originally written with numbered verses or chapters. This was accomplished along with various translations in order to have a reference method of finding and easily going back to a particular point in the writings. If you can, imagine the original writings being continuous strings of words without punctuation or individual sentences. The original text also did not have upper and lower case letters. It was all written in what we call capital or uppercase letters.

The Bible has been translated into over 2,000 languages. By comparison, the writings of Shakespeare have been translated into 50 languages. The Bible is currently the best-selling book in the world, of all time. As I stated, it was originally written in three different languages, Hebrew, Greek, and Aramaic. It was first translated into English around 1382 by John Wycliffe. Keep in mind when we refer to translations and translators we are talking about well-educated people in their fields. They took the painstaking time to verify and check each and every letter to ensure that no mistakes were made during any of these translations. Also, when copies were made, the process involved many people and hours to complete, with accuracy being of utmost priority. These writings were treated with reverence and treated as though they came directly from God to man, which they did. The copies have been studied by scholars from around the world who have devoted their entire lives to the subject. The percentage of differences found due to misspellings, omissions, etc., of copies found from around the world is so low that they make no major impact on the writings. None of these discrepancies affect any doctrine or contradict any main point of Christianity. The accuracy is estimated to be around 95% of all the text written with all the words and only minor misspellings or in differences of words used.

We do not have any "original" manuscripts available for the Bible or for any other ancient writing for that matter. In the New Testament, there are over 24,000 handwritten copies or portions thereof that now exist. This is by far many more in number than any other ancient writings. The second most available ancient manuscripts are from Homer's Iliad, with only around 640 manuscript copies available. Most ancient documents which still exist today have fewer than 25 copies available.

I would like to go into some of the manuscript areas in greater detail here, however by no means do I pretend to be a scholar on this subject. This will not be an exhaustive study of these details in any way. There is plenty of research out there which can be utilized to verify this area of my book. I encourage you to search for yourself in order to provide assurance of the facts. Check it out for yourself! The topic of translations as applied to the Bible covers a wide spectrum, but I think it is important to get an idea, at least a basic one, of where the Bible came from and how it got into today's language. Also, for the record, the Bible itself says that scripture was given to humankind and the authors were inspired by the Holy Spirit of God to write it down.

*Knowing this first, that no prophecy of Scripture
is of any private interpretation, for prophecy never
came by the will of man, but holy men of God spoke
as they were moved by the Holy Spirit.*
- 2 Peter 1:20, 21

Chapter Three
The Old Testament Writings

Most of the Old Testament was written around 1400 B.C. until approximately 400 B.C. The one author that most folks are familiar with, who wrote some of the "oldest" Old Testament, was Moses. We have copies of most of the Old Testament books which have been preserved from as early as 200 B.C. in what was discovered in the Dead Sea Scrolls. The Old Testament contains 39 separate books which were written primarily in the Hebrew language, with some books being written in Aramaic. The oldest Hebrew manuscripts of the Old Testament that are still in existence are included with the collection of Dead Sea Scrolls which date from around 200 B.C. to 70 A.D. These contain the entire book of Isaiah and portions of every other Old Testament book except the book of Esther. Stay with me now, as we are going to go through some information that may be a little bit on the "detail" side of things. But I feel is still important as we take the steps through these early writings.

A collection known as the Geniza Fragments, which are portions of the Old Testament written in Hebrew and Aramaic languages, were discovered in 1947. They were found in an old synagogue in Cairo, Egypt, and these dated from around 400 A.D.

There is a collection of what is known as the "Ben Asher Manuscripts" which came from five or six generations of the family of Ben Asher. They made copies of the Old Testament utilizing the "Masoretic Hebrew" text, dating to around 700 to 950 A.D.

There are two main versions of the "Masoretic Hebrew" text which are known as the "Aleppo Codex" and the "Codex Leningradensis." The Aleppo Codex version contains copies of the complete Old Testament and is dated to around 950 A.D. One-fourth of these copies were destroyed in the "anti-Jewish" riots in 1947. The Codex Leningradensis text is the complete Old Testament in Hebrew copied by the last family member of Ben Asher somewhere around A.D. 1008.

The Old Testament was first translated to Aramaic around 400 B.C. This translation is called the "Aramaic Targums" and it is widely used by the Jewish people. They first began to speak Aramaic while in their captivity in Babylon. This was completed in order to help them better understand the Old Testament in the language they commonly spoke at the time. In the first century Palestine of Jesus' day, Aramaic was still the most common spoken language.

Around 250 B.C., the Old Testament was translated into Greek and it was known as the "Septuagint". This sometimes carries the designation "LXX," the Roman numeral for 70. This was due to it being generally understood that at least 70 translators worked on the conversion from the Hebrew language into Greek. The Septuagint was also used by New Testament writers when they quoted from the Old Testament. This was also the most used translation by the early church.

The oldest Greek LXX translations of the Old Testament which are still in existence are known as the "Chester Beatty Papyri." They contain 9 Old Testament Books in the Greek Septuagint dating to around 100 to 400 A.D. Other translations that date to around 350 A.D. are the "Codex Vaticanus" and "Codex Sinaiticus." Each of these texts contain most of the entire Old Testament within the Greek Septuagint.

Prior to 1948 some of the earliest complete manuscripts of all the Old Testament books were dated to around 950 A.D. In 1947 there were some Bedouin shepherds searching the caves of Qumran. While in these hillsides surrounding the Dead Sea in Israel, they discovered assorted clay jars containing neatly rolled-up scrolls. This became one of the most, if not "the" most important archaeological discoveries of the twentieth century.

Between 1947 and 1956, scrolls and fragments of text from twelve different caves were unearthed and are now known as the Dead Sea Scrolls. Over 900 separate texts written in Hebrew, Aramaic, and Greek languages were found. This collection included every book of the Hebrew Bible except for Nehemiah and Esther. The longest biblical scroll was an almost complete text of the book of Isaiah. The Dead Sea Scrolls are approximately 2,000 years old and at least 1,000 years older than what had previously been considered the oldest manuscript copies of the Hebrew Bible. Another important finding discovered is that when you compare these two sets of text, they have very few variations. The fact is that these manuscripts written at least a thousand years apart in time are almost identical. They were verified to be word-for-word identical with the standard Hebrew Bible in more than 95% of the text. The 5% in variations were consisted of minor differences in the spelling of some words. This is absolute proof of the amazing accuracy of the Old Testament books which were preserved in a manner you can't just "shrug off."

What archaeologists discovered was not just one cave but 11 caves and they uncovered an entire library of writings from the Jewish community dating from the Second Temple period (approximately 516 B.C. – 70 A.D.). They found various books which contained commentaries along with other Biblical material that wasn't part of the Bible. These writings included at least parts of every single book of the Old Testament other than the book of Esther.

One the most interesting discoveries was an almost complete book of Isaiah. Scholars examined the Isaiah scroll and compared it to our earliest known copies of Isaiah that date to around 900 to 1000 A.D. They found that there were around 2,600 textual variations, with most differences considered minor such as spellings, order of words, and singular versus plural words. Isaiah Chapter 53 is considered prophecy which predicted the suffering and death of Jesus to come. The Dead Sea Scrolls offer more proof of the accuracy of the copies of text which were brought into the Bible.

They also offer more evidence that the people given the responsibility for copying biblical manuscripts took the utmost care in the details of their work. They knew they were working with God's word, so they took extraordinary steps to prevent any mistakes. These folks examined every part carefully before they put down any word or even a single letter. They strived to make sure without a doubt that everything was correct. I don't know if you know or not, but there were not any copy machines around when these texts were being copied. Trained and educated professional Jewish scribes would copy text by hand onto dried animal skins. Papyrus or paper wasn't developed until about 100 B.C.

As they were going through the copying process, they would check every letter carefully before they put it down. This was done to ensure accuracy and to prevent any mistakes from being written down. It was considered an honor to be chosen to perform these tasks and it was taken with the utmost seriousness. If a mistake was found, they didn't just erase the error, they would burn the bad copy and start over on a new one. So, you may wonder: What if the scribes carefully copied the text and burned the copies that had errors? Were there other methods utilized so they could copy the texts correctly? There were. One way to look at the history of the Old Testament is to make comparisons to other documents from the past.

For many of these comparisons we have around a thousand years between the actual writing of the document to when the first copy was discovered. There is the example of a Roman historian and politician named Publius Tacitus (56-120 A.D.). We have very few textual copies of his writings and these are dated to somewhere around 1100 A.D. He wrote these around 100 A.D., one thousand years before the copies were found. Most historians believe that we have a good idea of what Tacitus actually wrote down. This is true even though we only have partial or incomplete text and the earliest manuscript is dated one thousand years older than when the original writing occurred

The first textual copy of the Old Testament is dated from around 250 B.C. We got it about 150 years after the original book was written. The entire Old Testament was translated into Greek around 200 B.C., in a work known as the Septuagint. It can be seen from this translation that the complete Old Testament had been finished prior to this time. Remarkably, the writing is just about the same as it was during this time 2,200 years ago. This was just 200 years after the completion of the final Old Testament book!

The Old Testament was written from the time that Moses was alive from around 1400 B.C., through the time of Ezras' life around 400 B.C. There are some copies of most of the Old Testament books that have been preserved in the Dead Sea Scrolls from as early as 200 B.C. There are also many of the books that have been preserved from the ancient Cairo Geniza from around 100 A.D.

Codex Cairensis includes the books of the prophets and is dated to around 895 A.D. The Aleppo Codex includes most of the Old Testament and dates from around the 930's A.D. The oldest full Old Testament manuscripts which are in the Hebrew language is the "Leningrad Codex" from 1008 A.D., and are over 1,000 years old. We currently have over 10,000 Old Testament manuscripts. When compared together they have a remarkable accuracy unlike any other ancient writings known to exist on the planet.

So, what does all of this mean? I know it is a great deal of information and just think, I wanted to keep it short! So, in short, it means that regardless of what people say about the words of the Old Testament being corrupted, the idea doesn't hold water. The many facts should be considered such as the overwhelming number of accurate copies, the copying process, the Dead Sea Scrolls, and the many references made by the writers of the New Testament.

The Old Testament was written primarily in Hebrew with some books written in Aramaic. The following is a brief description in chronological order of how the writings came to us. We do not have any known autographs, which are the original writings of the books of the Old Testament. The approximate date generally accepted by scholars of 1450-1400 B.C., is for the writing of Genesis, Exodus, Leviticus, Numbers and Deuteronomy. These books were attributed to Moses as the author and were originally written in the Hebrew language.

Around 585 B.C., Jerusalem was destroyed by the Babylonian king Nebuchadnezzar and the Jewish people were taken into captivity to Babylon. They remained in Babylon under the Medo-Persian Empire and while there began to speak in Aramaic. The book of Daniel in verses 2:4 through 7:28 was written in Aramaic between 555-545 B.C. The last book of the Old Testament, Malachi, was written in Hebrew around 425 B.C. The book of

Ezra in verses 4:8 through 6:18 and verses 7:12-26 were written in Aramaic around 400 B.C.

The following is a partial list of the oldest Hebrew manuscripts which are still known to exist. The Dead Sea Scrolls mentioned earlier date from around 200 B.C. through 70 A.D. They contain the entire book of Isaiah and portions of every other Old Testament book except for the book of Esther.

The Geniza Fragments contain portions the Old Testament in Hebrew and Aramaic. They were discovered in 1947 at an old synagogue in Cairo, Egypt, and are dated from around 400 A.D. The Ben Asher Manuscripts from around 700-950 A.D. and were written by five or six generations of this family. They made copies of the Old Testament using the Masoretic Hebrew text of which we have at least two sets. The Aleppo Codex contained the complete Old Testament and is dated to around 950 A.D. Over one-fourth of this Codex was destroyed in the anti-Jewish riots which occurred in 1947. The Codex Leningradensis is a complete Old Testament version written in Hebrew that was copied by the last member of the Ben Asher family around 1008 A.D.

The first time we have record of God's word being written down was revealed to us in the book of Exodus. This event occurred when God wrote the Ten Commandments on stone tablets by His own finger. They were given to Moses near the peak of Mount Sinai. Biblical scholars date this occurrence to sometime around 1,500 B.C. or about 3,500 years ago. The language used at that time was most likely an ancient form of Hebrew.

The earliest scriptural text is most commonly referred to as the "Pentateuch." This set contains the first five books of the Bible which were believed to have been written by Moses. It contains the books of Genesis, Exodus, Leviticus, Numbers, and Deuteronomy. The original Old Testament scriptures were written in ancient Hebrew, a language much different than the Hebrew we have today which was passed down from generation to generation for thousands of years. When the entire Pentateuch is printed on a single scroll, it is called a "Torah" and the scroll completely unrolled is over 150 feet long. As we have seen in this last bit of information, the Old Testament is an amazingly preserved set of writings. In fact, there are no other ancient writings that even come close to being available in the number and accuracy of what we currently have. It would be impossible to put together this amount of information, scatter it all around the world, and for it to still be available with this amount of detail.

So, we have looked at some of the textual evidence, how many, how old, the limited number of errors in all of the copies, etc. Now how does this determine what was kept as part of the Bible or not? The early leaders, Rabbis and the scholars at that time put together the group of writings we know as the Old Testament. They did this by applying certain tests to them to see whether or not they were writings inspired by God. These tests were agreed upon and it was determined if they could be counted as part of the "canon" or list of writings that met all of their tests. As they looked at each potential document, they would apply these tests to it and if it passed, it would be accepted and included in the group of other writings.

The words of the Lord are pure words,
Like silver tried in a furnace of earth, Purified seven times.
- Psalms 12:6

CHAPTER FOUR
THE NEW TESTAMENT WRITINGS

This chapter will contain some of the evidence of where the New Testament writings came from and how they got to us. It is called the New Testament because its writings primarily contain the history of the life of Jesus Christ's time on earth. This part of the Bible also contains many references relating to the early church and the proper explanations of doctrine. It is important to note here that the word "church" is not referring any particular denomination, but as an actual group of people in the world who are considered believers and followers of Jesus Christ.

Autographs are defined as the original texts that were written either by the author's own hand or by a scribe that was under their supervision. There is much evidence today which presents the words of Christ that were written down and kept in what we could call notes or letters before they were copied over into the books which we have today. Until Johannes Gutenberg (1395-1468) first printed the Latin Bible in 1456, all Bibles were copied by hand utilizing papyrus, parchment, or paper. This was an accepted method of recording events that happened. They were compiled together to form the New Testament books which were kept and copied in an accurate and detailed method.

About 25% of the authorship of the New Testament is attributed to Paul. Paul was also named Saul and was from the city of Tarsus, which was located in Cilicia, a south-coastal region of Asia Minor at the time. He had the two different names due to Saul being his given Hebrew name and Paul as his Roman name because he was also a Roman citizen. There is a ton of information out there on Paul and for this book's purpose, I will not get into a lot of detail. In this section I will focus on some of the aspects of the evidence surrounding the writings.

The New Testament writings have been preserved in more copies of manuscripts than any other early literature that we have. We have over 5,800 complete or damaged Greek copies, and over ten 10,000 Latin manuscripts. There are also over 9,300 manuscripts available in other earlier languages which include Syriac, Slavic, Gothic, Ethiopic, Coptic and Armenian. The accuracy of the New Testament is supported by textual evidence which outshines any other written material known to humans.

It contains a total of 27 individual books which were written between 40 and 90 A.D. We have a fragment of the book of John that exists from around 125 A.D. The Greek manuscripts that we currently have are writings which can be used in providing accurate comparisons to other manuscripts. We can utilize these copies to put together an almost complete restoration of the oldest text.

The oldest complete New Testament text we have is known as the "Codex Sinaiticus." They can be dated to around the years 325 through 360 A.D. These texts reveal that these writings had been in circulation as a complete book for a long time. Even though the original manuscripts are no longer around, we have many copies which prove that the texts we have are accurate to the original written versions. There are in existence a total of over 25,000 partial and complete manuscript copies which are considered historic and preserved for our reference.

Taking into consideration the thousands of manuscripts available, we also have over 86,000 quotations dating from early church history. Also available are several thousand Lectionaries, which are church service books containing Scripture quotations that were used in the early years of Christianity. Early church leaders quite often quoted from these writings in their own documents.

If you could imagine for a bit that you don't have a copy of the Bible. Then, gather all of the quotations written down from the early church and put everything together, you would have an almost complete version of the whole New Testament. This would be comprised of material that was written from around 150 to 200 years after the life of Jesus Christ. Amazing, isn't it? There is an overwhelming amount of evidence that supports the reliability of the New Testament.

There have been around 200,000 variants or differences identified within the New Testament text that are contained in all of the sources. So, how do we view all of these variances or discrepancies in the text? How does it line up with our thinking that these writings are considered accurate? Were they indeed reproduced and brought down through history to us in a reliable method?

At first glance it seems like there are a lot of errors in these texts, right? If you take a look at what these variants are defined as, it will give you a clearer picture of what's going on. Most of them are as simple as misspelled words or even a missing single word in any of the over five 5,000 manuscripts available.

Johann Bengel (1687-1752) had a problem of sorts with the 30,000 or so variants that were brought out in what was released as the "Mill's Edition" of the Greek New Testament. He studied these discrepancies and found out that the variants were actually fewer in number than what it appeared to be on the surface and that none of them changed any major doctrine of Christianity.

Brooke Westcott (1825-1901) and John Hort (1828-1892) were translators who wrote in the 1870s that the New Testament text remains over 98% accurate. This accuracy held true no matter which text you utilized, either the "Textus Receptus" or the Greek text which was mostly derived from the "Codex Sinaiticus" and "Codex Vaticanus." When textual scholars examine all 5,600 Greek New Testament manuscripts, they find that they can group them into four text-types or families with other similar manuscripts.

There are many writings and records which come from sources other than the Bible that support events of the New Testament. We have thousands of quotations from writers in the early church between 100-450 A.D. They are accurate to the point of containing pretty much almost all of the New Testament. Along with this, we have recorded comments from several secular and Jewish historians in history. These include Tacitus

Aristides Epictetus (that's a mouthful!), Josephus, Lucian, Sueto-nius, and Pliny the Younger.

We have thousands of manuscript copies of the New Testa-ment and most scholars agree to having discovered more than 200,000 identified as "variants." That sounds like a great deal of discrepancies or mistakes to those of us not so educated in this field. The truth of the matter is that it is not what it seems. Out of 150,000 of these variants, 99% of them do not really make any sig-nificant issue with the writings. Some of them reversed the order of two words like "Jesus Christ" compared to "Christ Jesus." Other identified variants are only items that are missing a single letter in a particular word. Some of the differences are simply the absence of one or more minor words. Looking at all of these cases, they do not change any of the meanings or doctrines re-garding major theology issues within the books. When you ex-amine all of the facts, there are only around 50 possible variants which could be considered significant.

It is important to note that none of these discrepancies change or alter any major doctrine of the Christian faith. More than 99% of the original text writings can be reconstructed to a degree of accuracy unlike any other historical text from any other writers. As we look at all of the evidence, it clearly shows that the New Testament manuscripts are amazingly accurate and trustworthy. We have more manuscripts copied with greater accuracy from an earlier time than any other secular writings that may exist.

"If we compare the present state of the text of the New Testament with that of any other ancient

writing, we must...declare it marvelously correct."
Dr. Benjamin Warfield (1851-1921)

Close to the end of the First Century A.D., the New Testament had been completed. There are over 5,600 early Greek manuscripts that are still in existence. It was written in Greek and transcribed onto papyrus, a thin paper-like material that was made from long thin strips of a papyrus reed plant. The papyrus sheets were bound or tied together in a manner similar to the method of modern books that were later written on leather called "parchment."

The groupings or collections of papyrus were called a "codex." The oldest copies of the New Testament known to exist today are known as the "Codex Alexandrius" and the "Codex Sinaiticus" which are currently located in the British Museum Library in London, England. We have the copies of the "Codex Vaticanus" in the Vatican within Rome, Italy. These date to around 300 A.D.

Between 45 through 95 A.D., the New Testament was written in Greek. The letters from Paul as well as the books of Mark and Luke, along with the book of Acts were all written between 45 through 63 A.D. The books of John and the Revelation may have been written as late as 95 A.D. The New Testament manuscript which dates most closely to the original autograph was copied around 125 A.D., within 35 years of the original. It is named "p52" (the "p" meaning papyrus) and it contains a small portion of John Chapter 18. The Bodmer papyrus "p66" was written around 200 A.D., and is a manuscript which contains most of the book of

John. Also, from Bodmer, written around 225 A.D., is papyrus "p75" which contains the books of Luke and John.

From around 200 A.D., we have the Chester Beatty Biblical papyrus "p 46" which contains the letters from Paul and the book of Hebrews. Written between 250 through 300 A.D. is the Chester Beatty Biblical papyrus "p45" which contains portions of the books of Matthew, Mark, Luke and John as well as the book of Acts.

In 315 A.D. Athanasius the Bishop of Alexandria assembled the 27 books that we now include in what is called "the canon" of the New Testament. Written around 350 A.D., the Codex Sinaiticus text contains the entire New Testament and almost the entire Old Testament. It was discovered by a German scholar, Constantine Tischendorf, in 1844 at an Orthodox monastery located at Mt. Sinai in the Sinai Peninsula of Egypt. The Codex Vaticanus is very similar to the Sinaiticus text and dates also to around 350 A.D. It is an almost complete copy of the New Testament and was cataloged as being in the Vatican Library since 1475.

Early translations of the New Testament can reveal important information contained within the Greek manuscripts from which they were translated. Around 180 A.D., early translations came from the Greek language into the Latin, Syriac, and Coptic languages. Around 195 A.D., the name of the first translation of the Old and New Testaments from Greek into Latin was called "Old Latin." Parts of this Old Latin translation were discovered in quotes by Quintus Tertullian, an author, who lived between 155-220

A.D. in North Africa who wrote many treatises on theology. About 300 A.D., the "Old Syriac" translation was produced from the Greek language into the Syriac language. Around 380 A.D., Jerome, also known as "Jerome of Stridon" translated the New Testament from the original Greek language into Latin. This translation is commonly referred to as the "Latin Vulgate" version.

As you may have recognized in a great many of these details we have covered, these text and translations came to us "in steps." Imagine that someone was taking steps long before we ever got to see what we have today. I know this is a lot of information and I did not include it to intentionally overwhelm you. I only want to show an order and reference to how these important writings came to us. Remember, this is not in any manner a complete list of all of the text, nor a complete list of everything that had been accomplished throughout history. I only want to give you a taste of some of the items I personally felt important to bring out.

> "The interval, then, between the dates of original composition and the earliest extant evidence becomes so small as to be in fact, negligible, and the last foundation for any doubt that the Scriptures have come down to us substantially as they were written has now been removed. Both the authenticity and the general integrity of the books of the New Testament may be regardedas finally established."
> Sir Frederic G. Kenyon (1863-1952)

Most scholars believe that many of the New Testament books were written by eyewitnesses. The book of John is said to have been written by the disciple of Jesus. Recent archeological research has confirmed the existence of the "Pool of Bethesda" and that it had five porticoes exactly as described in the book of John, Chapter 5, verse 2. This is just one instance of a detail that proves that the Book of John was written by John. He was an eyewitness that knew Jerusalem before it was destroyed in 70 A.D.

The apostle Paul personally signed his letters or epistles and he wrote them to churches that knew and were familiar with him. These churches were able to verify that these letters had come from him. Clement was an associate of Paul who wrote to the Corinthian Church in 97 A.D. asking them to make sure they listened to and followed the instructions that Paul had sent them.

There are many facts that provide reliable information that the Books of Luke and Acts were written prior to 65 A.D. This gives credibility to the author, Luke, and his testimony to being an eyewitness to Paul's missionary journeys. This would also date the writing of the Book of Mark before 65 A.D., and the letters from Paul between the years of 49-63 A.D.

The Book of Acts records the beginning history of the church. Again, the word "church" here is referring to the group of believers in Christ, not a particular denomination as such. Three different men. Peter, Paul, and James the brother of Jesus, are all mentioned in various roles throughout the book. They were all martyred or killed by 67 A.D., but their deaths are not recorded in the Book of Acts. The local church in Jerusalem played a major role in this book but the destruction of the city around 70 A.D., was not mentioned. This book ends with Paul under house arrest in the city of Rome in 62 A.D. Around 64 A.D., Nero, the Roman emperor, blamed and also persecuted Christians for the fire that destroyed the city of Rome. Paul himself was killed by 65 A.D., in the city of Rome and none of the persecution of the Christians in Rome or Paul's execution are mentioned.

The earliest manuscripts we have of major portions of the New Testament date from between 175-250 A.D. The early church leaders between 97-180 A.D., reference earlier manuscripts by quoting from all of them except for one of the books. Clement of Rome (35-99 A.D.) wrote a letter to the Corinthian Church around 97 A.D. In this he reminded them to pay attention to the letter that Paul had written to them years before. Clement also worked with Paul and he also quoted from the books of Luke, Acts, Romans, 1 Corinthians, Ephesians, Titus, 1st and 2nd Peter, Hebrews, and James.

The early church leaders Ignatius (30-107 A.D.), Polycarp (65-155 A.D.), and Papias (70-155 A.D.) all quoted verses from every book except 2nd and 3rd John. By these quotations they authenticated almost all of the entire New Testament. Ignatius and Polycarp were also disciples of the apostle John.

Justin Martyr (110-165 A.D.) referenced verses from the books of Matthew, Mark, Luke, John, Acts, Romans, 1 Corinthians, Galatians, 2nd Thessalonians, Hebrews, 1st and 2nd Peter, and Revelation. Irenaeus, (120-202 A.D.) wrote a 5-volume set of papers called "Against Heresies" to counter the false doctrines of gnostic sects. He quoted from every book of the New Testament over 1,200 times, except for John 3.

I will try in this part to briefly explain the term "canon" of scripture. The biblical description is a collection of the books that contain the scripture found in the Christian Bible. The writings had to measure up. The texts were given certain tests to make sure they met the criteria that would fall into what they considered legitimate or true scripture. As long as the writings met these tests, they were included in what we currently have in the "canon" of scripture or the complete Bible as we have it.

How was the New Testament canon determined? The early church had three main criteria for determining which books were to be included or excluded from the Bible. Number one, the books must have apostolic authority. Apostles were considered eyewitnesses or those that accompanied Christ during His lifetime on earth. Secondly, they had to have conformity to what was called the "rule of faith." In other words, the document had to agree with the truth or doctrine of the basic Christian tenets that the church recognized. Thirdly, there was the question of whether a document or text had been continually accepted and used by the church at large.

And you will seek Me and find Me,
when you search for Me with all your heart.
- Jeremiah 29:13

CHAPTER FIVE
THE WHOLE BOOK

In this section I will attempt to fill in some more gaps in the information on this book that we call "the Bible." For one thing, the Bible as we now have it available in many very truthful and accurate translations, can be rightfully considered the very word of God. As you read earlier, we have an amazing number of manuscripts, unlike any other old writings that give us the complete revelation of truths of the originals. And again, most of the textual variations are items such as spelling, word order and tenses do not have any major effect on any doctrine in any form.

We also need to remember that the overwhelming number of manuscripts we possess should greatly lower the margin of error when it comes to having what was written in the original documents. This is accomplished through applying the principle of what is known as" textual criticism." It can be briefly explained as simply comparing all of the available manuscripts we have. If we do that, we can almost guarantee that what we have available to us today is as close to having exactly what the original documents said as we can get.

When we just look at the discoveries of the Dead Sea Scrolls, the evidence provided regarding the Old Testament is accomplished with very few discrepancies. You can depend on this as a "word for word" copy that was originally inspired by God, given to mankind to record, and supernaturally preserved for us to read today. If you look at all of this and include the extraordinary amount of textual evidence we have for the New Testament, you can confidently say without hesitation that this book of books, "the Bible" is truly remarkable. I know, I know, people argue with me all of the time about how this book just can't be real because it's too old. The old saying is true-- "you can lead a horse to water, but you can't make him drink." I guess you can't convince folks of things they just don't want to believe, no matter what the evidence.

History shows us that one of the reasons we now have the English language Bible is that it comes from the story of the "Protestant Reformation" which began in the late 14th century A.D., by John Wycliffe (1328-1384). The study of the Protestant Reformation would certainly be worth pursuing and I would encourage you, the reader, to dig into this critical part in the history of the church. Hebrew and English languages are both considered what they call "picture languages" as the very words can form a clear picture in your mind. The first man to ever print the scriptures translated from the original language into English was William Tyndale (1494-1536). He quoted Jerome of Stridon in saying, "Saint Jerome also translated the Bible into his mother tongue. Why may we not also? They will say it cannot be translated into our tongue because it is so rude. It is not that our tongue is rude, but that they are false liars because the Greek tongue agrees more with English than with Latin. And the properties of the Hebrew tongue agree a thousand times more with English than with Latin."

William Tyndale was qualified, if anyone was, to make such a statement because he was fluent in eight different languages. It was said that you could have thought any one of them to be his native tongue. He was an amazing person and was put to death by being burned on a stake for completing his work of translating the Bible. This makes for a huge statement on dedication to a cause. I would suggest for further study, that you explore the information and books available out there on William Tyndale.

The following is a brief list in chronological order of translations of the Bible. As the Bible is translated into a different language it is most often translated from the original Hebrew and Greek. Some of the earlier translations in the past were completed by utilizing an earlier version in a different language. For example, the first English translation by John Wycliffe (1328-1384) and completed around 1380 was prepared from the Latin Vulgate language.

Around 180 A.D., the first translations of the New Testament were completed from Greek into Latin, Syriac, and Coptic languages. Around 195 A.D. the first translation of the Old and New Testaments into Latin was named "Old Latin," There have been parts of the Old Latin which were found in quotes by Quintus Tertullian (160-220 A.D.) in north Africa. Around 300 A.D. the "Old Syriac" translation of the New Testament was compiled from the Greek language into Syriac. This time period also brought forth Coptic Versions which were translated into and spoken in four different dialects around Egypt.

In 380 A.D., the "Latin Vulgate" version, translated by Jerome into Latin encompassed the Old Testament which derived from Hebrew and the New Testament deriving from Greek. The Latin Vulgate became the main Bible of the Western Church until the time of the Protestant Reformation. The Reformation brought about many different translations of the Bible into common known languages of the people during that time.

In 1380 A.D., John Wycliffe (1328-1384) produced the first English translation of the Bible from the Latin Vulgate. He was a scholastic philosopher, theologian, biblical translator, reformer, priest, and a seminary professor at the University of Oxford. He was considered to have an important role at this time in history called the "Protestant Reformation." Note that this was not completed from the original Hebrew and Greek languages.

In 1456 A.D., Johannes Gutenberg, a German craftsman and inventor of the printing press, "printed" the first Bible in Latin. In 1514 A.D., Erasmus of Rotterdam (1455-1536) produced the Greek New Testament which was taken from 5 Greek manuscripts, the oldest of which dated to around the twelfth century. These Greek manuscripts later became known as the "Textus Receptus" or the "received texts." Around 1520 A. D., the "Polyglot Bible" was completed with the Old Testament books written in Hebrew, Aramaic, Greek, and Latin and the New Testament written in Greek and Latin. Erasmus made use of the Polyglot text to revise later copies of the New Testament.

In 1525 A.D., William Tyndale (1494-1536) produced the first incomplete translation of the Bible from the original text into the English language. He also used the Polyglot Bible for references in this translation of the Old Testament. He was not able to completely finish the translation because he was martyred in 1534.

Around 1560 the Geneva Bible was printed and it was the first English language Bible that added numbered verses to each chapter. This Bible was machine-printed and made available to the general public. It was widely used by many people for a number of years.

The original "King James Version" was completed in 1611 A.D., from the original Hebrew and Greek languages. The translators of the New Testament utilized the Textus Receptus text for their translations.

In 1769, the Oxford Standard Edition, which was a carefully revised copy of the 1611 King James Version was completed.

In 1833 Noah Webster's Bible was printed, offering his own revision of the King James Bible.

In 1901 The American Standard version was made available as the first major "American" revision of the King James Version.

In 1973 The New International Version was published as a "modern and accurate phrase-for-phrase English translation" of the Bible.

The version known as "The New King James Version" was

published in 1979 and a completed Bible made available in 1982.

This version was made as an update with vocabulary and grammar to reflect the English language as spoken today.

As you can see, the number of copies and translations that have been made in recent years has increased. I only listed some of the translations as they have come to us in order to give an idea of the history of the Bible. I did not include or exclude any particular versions for any reason other than just trying to limit the length of this list.

There are over 2,800 versions of the Bible now available in around 2,000 different languages. While it is impossible to know the exact number, the estimates range somewhere between 5 and 7 billion copies of the Bible being produced and it is the best-selling book of all time.

In other words, there have been many translations completed since these early versions were done. I am not going to list all of them going forward from this point, but I do want to mention the fact that there are some very good translations out there. In my opinion there are also what I believe to be some "not so good" translations as well. Some of them are not technically translations, but they are paraphrases or revisions which line up with some particular individual or individuals thoughts or ideas. So, this is where you need to do your homework and check out the versions that are available. Note where and how they came about and seek this information from reliable sources. There are plenty of great resources available.

I mean this in all sincerity because there are some outright "corrupt" versions available. They have not taken the text we have available and properly translated it either on purpose or they used people who are not trained in these languages at all. Some bad versions are due to "religions" forming so-called translations into material that fit their particular needs. As I said, there are some very good translations which are based on reliable textual writings. They have been produced by biblical scholars which have spent the better part of their entire lives in this type of work. As in any subject, you have to be careful of deliberate misinterpretations which are out there and then apply careful investigation. Remember, just because it's on the internet doesn't make it true!

I have given this brief history not to boggle your mind with details but to at least demonstrate factual evidence of how the Bible came to us. There have been many books written on the people, times, methods and archaeology relating to the reliability of the writings of the Bible. My biggest point in all of this is to give you something to build upon and hopefully stir an interest into discovering for yourself.

I would like to take a few moments to talk about some of the other books you may have heard of which are texts which are considered history but not necessarily considered inspired books given to us by God. A few centuries before the birth of Christ, the Jewish historical books known as the "Apocrypha" were completed and written in Greek. Jerome had recorded in a note adjacent to the Apocrypha books that he did not know whether or not they were inspired scripture or just Jewish historical writings.

The Apocrypha books were retained as part of most every Bible (handwritten or printed) from the early days until around 120 years ago, in the mid-1880s, when they were removed from Protestant Bibles. These books were believed to be a part of the Bible even though there was not agreement on whether they were inspired by God.

There is nothing found in history to indicate that the Apocrypha is only a "Roman Catholic" thing. The Roman Catholics kept 12 of the 14 Apocrypha Books in their Bible even though the Protestants removed all of them. By around 500 A.D., the Bible had been translated into over 500 languages, but by around 600 A.D., it had been allowed in only one language, Latin Vulgate. The only organized and recognized church at that time in history was the Catholic Church of Rome and they did not allow scripture to be produced in any language other than Latin. This rule was put into effect in order for the church to officially instruct because the priests were for the most part educated to understand Latin (most other folks couldn't) and this gave the church more authority. People who were caught with and had in their possession non-Latin scriptures would be executed. The thousand-year period from around 400 A.D. to 1400 A.D., was known as the "Dark and Middle Ages" and lasted until what led up to the Protestant Reformation.

So, how can we trust the manuscript evidence that we have? As with any writings that were transmitted through a number of handwritten manuscripts, it is natural to ask the question, "how can we really know that we have anything resembling the original writing or autograph?" We have already looked at the evidences we have for the reliability of the New Testament manuscripts. In comparison, let's look at a few early manuscripts of other writings besides the Bible and how they line up as far as the number of copies and the time they were written.

Tacitus, the Roman historian, wrote his "Annals of Imperial Rome" around 115 A.D. Only one manuscript of this work remains to this day and it was copied around 850 A.D. If you look at Plato and his work, there are around 250 known manuscripts available and they are dated to over 1,250 years after the original writing.

Josephus, the Jewish historian, wrote "The Jewish War" shortly after 70 A.D. There are nine manuscripts available in Greek which date from between 1000-1200 A.D., and one Latin translation from around 400 A.D.

The earliest known surviving text of Buddha is 29 scrolls which were first written down around 500 years after his death. Homer's "Iliad" was written around 800 B.C. This was considered as important to ancient Greeks as the Bible was to the Hebrew people. There are only around 650 manuscripts available and they date from around 200-300 A.D. This is well over 1,000 years after it was originally written.

The earliest copies of Julius Caesar's works are available from around 950 years after they were originally written and includes around 75 manuscripts.

What we see is that when you look at other ancient texts and consider the relationship of time between the actual events, the date of writing, and the earliest known manuscript copies we have, you see a major difference in reliability. One manuscript of a portion of the Gospel of Matthew (the Magdalen text) is dated around 200 A.D., which was only around 160 years after the crucifixion of Jesus Christ took place. The time between the actual historical events and when the writings took place is much closer for the New Testament than any other ancient manuscripts we have.

This is the first step of looking at the truth of where the ancient writings concerning God came from. It is an all important step as we build on the evidence of where and how the writings came to humankind from God. These letters or books that were brought forth from thousands of years ago are in a way an introduction, or a beginning to understand who God is. To bring out a few important truths to the writings we call "scripture" is a major starting step. One of these truths is that God had the power and the authority to inspire His words to humankind. After all, if He was the one who created everything, the universe, stars, planets and humans, He certainly has and had this overall power. And secondly, if He had the power to inspire these original words, He most certainly had the power to preserve these writings in absolute detail for the future generations to read. Since we have so many copies of reliable manuscripts, this proves the preservation that took place. This is what is called "supernatural" as it defies all of the natural laws that we have come to understand.

You can look at the Bible itself for the evidence that is illustrated within its text. If we examine the New Testament writings, we can see how Christ himself referenced the Old Testament many times. He knew that what He was referencing was accurately and faithfully preserved throughout the times. There were no errors mentioned by Him concerning any of these older references. They were quoted directly as they were written, leading us to conclude the words He was quoting were the correct representation of the originals, this being the word of God. Jesus and his apostles all realized that God had brought forth these copies and translations in a manner that could be trusted just as much as the originals themselves.

You see, there is overwhelming evidence that the Bible is the most documented, accurately copied, preserved group of writings handed down through time to which mankind has access. This is the first step. It is starting out and building on the foundation to something that must have been placed here on earth for our reference and understanding. It absolutely can be trusted in order to take that first step. It's not blind faith, but something that can be depended on like a solid concrete foundation with iron rods to strengthen its core for whatever will be built upon it. Take with me this first step in full assurance and let us continue with the journey that is before us.

"The Bible does not thrill; the Bible nourishes.
Give time to the reading of the Bible and the recreating
effect is as real as that of fresh air physically." [2]

PART TWO:
THE SECOND STEP -
THE STORIE(S)

TAKING A CLOSER LOOK
AT WHAT'S INSIDE

*All Scripture is given by inspiration of God, and is
profitable for doctrine, for reproof, for correction,
for instruction in righteousness, that the
man of God may be complete, thoroughly
equipped for every good work.*
- II Timothy 3:16,17

CHAPTER SIX:
THIS BOOK OF BOOKS

Ok, so here we are at the second step in this process that we are undergoing, taking a closer look at what's inside. I don't know if you noticed or not, but in the first step or part of the book, there were many smaller steps contained within it. As I have stressed throughout this book, life as we know it is full of steps and the idea of taking these steps is central to this work.

We have taken a look at many details of the original textual evidence. There is overwhelming evidence that we can depend on as the groundwork for having these remarkable stories available in order to learn about God. Now, as we take our second step in the series, we will take a look at the entirety of the Bible and delve just a bit into each individual book. Keep in mind that I am only offering a small "tidbit" of information concerning each one of these important writings. If you're ready to go with me, come on and let's take the next step into this journey.

In this section, I will attempt to cover some of the details of each of the books of the Bible. For the purpose of this book, I don't want us to get too involved in the many stories that are within them. I want to encourage you as the reader to explore the writings of this book on your own, in your own time, studying to seek out the truth that lies within. It is filled with so much information that volumes and volumes of study guides and information are available; so much that we cannot possibly cover it all in this reading.

The Bible is a book that contains science, history and prophecy of things to come. The science within the Bible is not the purpose of the Bible, but it is still part of it. Much of it was written before people really understood things such as the Earth being round. The history, events, and things that have happened over time have been proven and archaeological evidence has continued to verify much of the Bible.

Every sentence in the Bible is important and the books are richly filled with words containing information that can enlighten the reader as no other writings can do. I have personally experienced the reading of certain scriptures and did not have any real revelation or understanding. Then at another time, going over the same writings, they explode with light reaching deep into my soul. It not only happens to me, there are many Bible scholars and everyday people who have experienced the same thing. This book is like no other found on the earth. It was inspired by God and given to us by inspiration to men who wrote the words down that we have today. I don't want you to read my short descriptions and think that's all there is to it.

There are many excellent study guides available such as the "Matthew Henry Bible Commentary" which gives a sentence-by-sentence explanation. The "Strong's Exhaustive Concordance" is great for studying the Bible's original languages as you can search particular words and find their many uses throughout the entire Bible. Both of these tools are available for free on-line. You can also use these references utilizing several available translations of the Bible. These are just two of the resources available and I encourage you to seek out other sources that will help you in your journey exploring the word of God.

Unlike other books, the Bible is not just divided into chapters, but is actually divided into smaller books. Each book has its own writer (or writers) and one (or more) general subject matters within it. Sometimes it is about things that have already happened in the past, things that are happening at the time, or things that are going to happen in the future. Or they can contain all of these in one book. Just keep in mind that whatever the story content, it's not just revealed to us for the story's sake, but it has a much deeper overall meaning. Each book comes from men who were inspired by God to write content down for references to humankind. Some of them are like letters from God to us for instruction or to help us understand His very nature. Each book is a mini or smaller book that references particular times within the writings that allows us to see how God operated and how He expects us to operate. But most of all, and most importantly, it helps us move forward in our relationship with Him.

On the method of us taking steps, I believe that God is a step-taker Himself. We are told in the beginning with the book of Genesis that on the first day God created, on the second day God created, on the third day God created and so it goes for creation itself. God took steps with making the universe. The Bible says

He took six days and that included making us humans.

From the beginning God as the great "step-taker" created humans in His image, so guess what? We're step-takers just like God. Also, in Genesis, we can find where God was walking in the garden because Adam heard Him walking there. Taking steps, oh my, we take steps too! Step-taking is just what you're doing by reading this book.

I once heard a simple description of the Bible as "the Old Testament can be looked at as letters or stories about God, His nature, the way He operated with humans, and about who He is." What's known as the gospel books (first four) of the New Testament are directly related to the life of Jesus Christ. They cover the time from His birth through His childhood, His ministry, and eventually His death and resurrection. The rest of the New Testament is mostly describing the Holy Spirit of God. These books reveal the impact and work within the lives of believers while following Christ. There will be more to come on this later, but I always thought this was a good brief description of the Bible.

The Bible was inspired as a "God creation" and it was given to us by God and it came to us by His direction. God revealed these books and the stories for our enlightenment, even today. These scriptures were kept divinely throughout history, as you have seen earlier in this book. There is no other book like it in the world. No other book comes close to having copies without error of so much writing.

The Bible is one of the best references to explain itself. Many questions concerning the material within the Bible can be explained within the Bible itself. You don't have to really go to any other sources, simply look at what the Bible says about itself. The Bible is not written in chronological order and with regard to time; there may be huge spans between even verses or chapters. Also, remember the Bible was not written with chapter and verse numbers. They were assigned verses and chapter numbers later to provide an easier way to reference them. The entire Bible consists of 66 books written by around 40 different authors, 39 in the Old Testament and 27 in the New Testament.

This next section will be a brief outline of the Bible, beginning with the Old Testament and then the New Testament. I repeat, this is not going to be an exhaustive study. You can do that on your own. I just want to give a brief description and highlight some of the books that are located within this book of books known as the Bible. My hope is that this will pique your interest so you will want to explore further. There are many great study guides and Bibles available out there to peruse.

Again, in the following information I am trying to offer is in no way a complete study or revelation of what is contained within the scripture. These are brief descriptions containing only portions of each of these books because they contain so much more information than I am able to provide in this work. I recommend that you do your own study as you grow, and go further and deeper into the revealing nature of these writings.

Some of the English translations of certain words taken from the original writing in Hebrew or Greek can be imprecise. This is because there are really no proper English words for the translations. But going deeper in the original languages with available study guides can guide you through every single verse and word in the Bible.

As we continue our journey to take this next step or part of the book, we will look at the entire Bible. The first part of this step is broken down within the five chapters, 7-11, that cover divisions or selections of books in the Old Testament. As we build these divisions it will help to make it all easier to understand. Breaking the Bible down into smaller pieces or steps is one method to reduce the so-called "confusion" that many people speak of when it comes to the Bible. This helps in our journey by taking these smaller steps towards getting the bigger picture of the entire book. As you will see, most folks agree that by utilizing this method, it will make it much easier to understand. Are you ready? Let's go forward into this next step!

"You were placed on earth to know God.
Everything else is secondary."
Pastor Greg Laurie

Chapter Seven:
The Five Scrolls

As stated earlier, there are 39 books that are now considered the Old Testament part of the Bible. They were completed before 500 B.C., and were preserved in the Hebrew language on scrolls.

This first section of the Old Testament is known as "The Pentateuch or Law" and it includes the first five books of the Bible which are Genesis, Exodus, Leviticus, Numbers, and Deuteronomy. The literary category of the Pentateuch maintains the traditional Jewish grouping of these books together as the Torah. The Pentateuch was also the first collection of literature acknowledged as Scripture by the Hebrew community.

This Greek expression means "five scrolls" and was made popular by the Alexandria Jews in the first century A.D., who were under the influence of Greek culture. The Hebrew-speaking Jewish community referred to these five books as "The Law," "Torah," or "The Law of Moses."

The writing of these books has been attributed to Moses. Also, they are held in the highest respect as they contain the descriptions of the beginning of the earth as well as the creation of man.

GENESIS

The name Genesis refers to "beginnings" as this book gives a history of the beginning of the universe, the earth, the animals, and humankind. It also includes the history of what happened to the early human race in their relationship to God. The first 11 chapters cover a period of time that is at least equal to around 2,000 years and it could possibly be much longer. Chapters 12-50 cover a period of time around 350 years.

This book covers so much information and sets the stage for the rest of the books of the Bible. It gives inspired testimony from God to the writer, Moses, and allows him to write down the entire history of the beginning of creation. Scholars estimate that Moses wrote this book around 1,500 B.C. It is said to be a book of generations of forming the heavens and earth, and also of mankind from Adam and Eve through Noah, and down through the generations of Jacob.

This book is referred to over and over in the New Testament by the writers of those books. Overall, this established the authority given to this writing as extremely important to the Jewish people. God was a step-taker Himself. What is told in Genesis is that on the first day God created, on the second day God created, on the third day God created, and so it went for the days of the week. The writings reveal that He took steps in creating as he created certain things on one day, and the next day he created other things until everything was created, including humankind. God created for six days and then on the seventh day, He rested. Not that God needed to rest, but He gave us an example for us to follow because we need a rest day after working all week. It is important for human beings to take a break and to not overwork our bodies. The seven-day week which started in the beginning continues as a standard around the world.

From the beginning God, who is the step-taker, created man in His image and guess what? We are step-takers just like God. Also, in this book we find where God was walking in the garden because Adam heard him. By simply reading this book, you're taking steps. Some of what we have in Genesis describes history concerning the formation of the world and creation of humans. He did it in a specific order as he created everything on the planet. Now, if these steps weren't taken in the order that they were, the earth would not be supporting the animals and plants because it wouldn't have worked if they had been created in a different order. Again, God takes steps just like we do amazing, isn't it? We are indeed created in His image.

Genesis is so full of information as it covers the beginning of the universe and of the earth, and it describes the creation of humans. As part of His creation, the importance of the relationship between God and humans is shown and demonstrated within these writings. It shows that from the beginning, humankind had everything needed in life provided for by God. Although they had everything, they still could not keep the one rule that God gave them to obey. It comes down to obedience and shows that the problem started from the beginning, and we still have that same problem today. There are other illustrations that provide insight into how humankind is determined to operate without

God's direction. Remember that these stories told as literal stories, and are not just made up to demonstrate some point. Instead, they are based on real people and their inability to keep their part of the relationship properly.

EXODUS

Exodus has been referred to as the sequel to the book of Genesis, or the continuation of the story written by Moses. The word *exodus* means the "way out." This book focuses on the way out for the people of Israel from their captivity in Egypt. It also gives some information about the life of Moses growing up and becoming God's chosen man. The Ten Commandments are given in here, along with the organization of the temple as a place to meet with God. The temple is a picture of God's continuing determination to fellowship with man even though the relationship was broken by man. God made a new way to bridge this gap in the relationship through a temporary temple that God where would meet man. The blood sacrifices that were required were only temporary sacrifices for the eventual coming of the only sacrifice that would forever pay the penalty for humankind, Jesus Christ.

LEVITICUS

The name of this book is a meaning relating to the Levites, the tribe of Israel where the priests came from. This book not only deals with the special services of the Levites, but also gives detailed direction from God on the form of worship to take place, including sacrifices and the order or the way that they are to be carried out. The underlying message in this book teaches that the way to God is through sacrifice. The early sacrifices of animals and their blood was key. As humans disobeyed God in the garden, the way to reestablish the fellowship with Him was by sacrifice. Walking with Him requires holiness to be in sync with God. This book contains many symbols and references to the coming of the ultimate sacrifice for humankind in Christ Jesus. As you see in this book as well as many others within the Bible, God required certain steps be taken in the manner of worship. God is a God of order and the details in this book verify that God requires attention to the details for us to be obedient.

NUMBERS

The book of numbers gets its name from the census that was taken in the first chapter as well as one taken in the twenty-sixth chapter. The children of Israel departed from Mount Sinai and they were to go to a land that God had promised them. They had an attitude of unbelief and this later turned into disobedience. This should have been focused on their faith, but they failed. They were tested and failed, so they were not able to cross into the promised land. I think sometimes we fail the test as well, and we don't get the best that God had offered us. They had to wander in the desert until the whole generation died off except for Joshua and Caleb. This shows that God required obedience, and He would not fail to punish those who disobey, even His special people.

DEUTERONOMY

This book was written as Moses was nearing the end of his life and the people of Israel were waiting to cross the river Jordan into the land that they were promised. It reinforces the laws that were given to the people after nearly forty years of experience wandering in the wilderness. They had new problems and situations that surfaced which were not covered initially by the law. The emphasis on much of Deuteronomy is about the love of God and these principles concerning the peoples' obedience. The word "love" occurs 22 times and the word "obey" is used ten times in this one book. God requires obedience and He put forth these important rules for the people to follow. Moses gives his final instructions here before giving up his leadership position as he is about to approach death. The generation left here after wandering in the desert doesn't really relate to what the other older generation had been through. That kind of sounds familiar, doesn't it? I don't believe the young people in this country really relate to what the previous generations have gone through and done in the past. I believe it is important to understand and learn history so you will know what the previous generations did.

So God created man in His own image;
in the image of God he created him,
male and female He created them.
- Genesis 1:27

CHAPTER EIGHT
IT'S IN THE HISTORY

This next set of 12 books, consisting of Joshua, Judges, Ruth, 1 & 2 Samuel, 1 & 2 Kings, 1 & 2 Chronicles, Ezra, Nehemiah and Esther, are commonly known as the "Historical Books." These books share a prophetic story of history describing how the obedience or disobedience of God's people (the nation of Israel) is directly tied to blessings or curses. In the Hebrew arrangement, Joshua, Judges and the books of Samuel and Kings are also known as a group of books referred to as "the Former Prophets" due to the prophetic view from which they are written.

JOSHUA

The writer of this book is attributed to Joshua, the successor to Moses. The word Joshua means "Jehovah is salvation." It's the same word in the New Testament as Jesus. This book is to some people offensive due to the nature of war described. You must understand that it must be taken in the context of the history of the nation. They were trying to get to the land which they were promised to inherit by God, and not just a country trying to conquer and kill for the sake of taking. Remember, the people had come out of slavery under the nation of Egypt and God had chosen and directed them to this place to live and rest. Joshua dies at the end of this book after giving the people a reminder of how God has taken care of them throughout. He instructed them to hold fast to God and keep his covenant, and that God will not put up with disobedience.

JUDGES

The author of this book, while unknown, is generally accepted to be Samuel, having written at least part of it. This time of the Israeli people was after the death of Joshua. They had gone into the promised land and did not have a human leader, and God was their king. The promises of God had been fulfilled as they were in the land that had been given them. They quickly lost sight of the fact that they were chosen and were God's people, part of an emerging kingdom. As they were surrounded by the land of Canaan and the people, they started accepting and practicing their morals, gods and religious beliefs. In other words, they started living like their neighbors and took on their surroundings instead of staying true to God.

This book also contains the story of Samson, a familiar story to many people even if they don't know much about the Bible. Samson's life was, in a way, the very picture of how people behaved and still do today. People receive the blessings of God and then turn to disobedience and cry out to God for mercy. They did what was right in their own eyes by not following the directions given by God. When people live this way, as history has shown, it doesn't work out well. They had no human king, but several people acted as judges and attempted to lead the people. The problem of this hard-headed bunch was they just didn't want to accept the Lordship of God and they wanted to do the things that made them feel good. Nations have gone through these cycles as they serve God, then they slowly begin to do evil abandoning God. After that, they go into slavery of some form and become servants to that master until they cry out to God. They turn back to God and repent, are delivered, and then start serving God again; and the cycle continues. It is repeated many times throughout history. Sound familiar?

RUTH

Ruth was the great grandmother of David and was also listed in the human ancestry of Jesus. There is one other book in the Bible that is named after a woman and that is Esther. This book is said to be a love story. Although the word "love" is not mentioned, it is very much understood. It contains important genealogy which includes the link between the tribe of Judah and David. Its records are also found listed in the book of Matthew in the New Testament. This story can be viewed as an overall picture or representation of Christ and the relationship with His church. It is a short book, but contains the interactions between individuals and their great love for one another. They are willing to "think outside of the box" and carry on with their lives based on commitment and obedience, which by some people would be considered difficult. As in many of the books of the Bible, there is a tremendous amount of insight available to the reader within these writings.

1ST SAMUEL

This book is recognized as being written by Samuel, a person that God used to establish a monarchy in Israel. Samuel appointed Saul and David as Israel's first two human kings. He has been compared to Moses as an individual that provided a transition path forward for the people of Israel. First and Second Samuel were originally one book, but they were later divided into two parts by the translators. This book outlines Samuel's birth and his calling by God to be a prophet. Israel was defeated by the Philistines and the "ark of the covenant" was taken from them. After God's wrath was directed against the Philistines, it was returned to them.

The first kingship of Saul began here, though not really approved of by God, but instead chosen by the people. Saul's character was not quite what it needed to be. After the reign of Saul came the establishment of David as King of Israel.

2ND SAMUEL

The second part of the Book of Samuel continues the message which is in the first book and it provides details concerning the entire reign of David as king. David is listed in the human lineage as an ancestor of Jesus and he was considered somewhat of an ideal king, even though he had his own issues just like every one of us. David had much success as king of God's people. But again, just like all of us, David was a human and had his own troubles. In a way, he would ask God to look the other way while he did what he wanted to. We all do that, don't we?

1st Kings

This book is one of the three sets of books that were originally written as one book. The division of this book was completed by the early pre-Christian Greek translators of the Old Testament. First Kings details the death of king David and then begins with the era of king Solomon. After Solomon, it then continues through the many kings that the nation of Israel had over time. One of the teachings found here is that man himself has trouble ruling even himself in the world. This book also describes some of the divisions of the kingdom of Israel as well revealing prophecy that became fulfilled. The writer references occasions that king David was considered a standard by which the other kings would be measured. God also showed that He had amazing grace, in that revival would come when the king and the people would turn back to Him.

It is shown that the leaders on earth, when in tune with heaven, receive blessings and benefits. But our human plans will not overcome God's ultimate purposes. In other words, it is by far much better to try and stay in step with God as our Heavenly Father and follow his path for our lives. It is not that God is a mean controller, but He only wants the best for us. Remember that He knows the future so as a loving father to His children, the relationship is all-important.

2nd Kings

This book continues the stories that had begun in First Kings. It establishes kings and prophets as the path of communication with God instead of going through the priest. The captivity of the nation of Israel by Assyria is recorded and was actually permitted by God for three basic reasons. God repeated His specific directions to the people to turn from their evil ways and keep His commandments, which they did not do. Secondly, they became hard-headed and did not want to listen, just like some of the previous people. What it comes down to is that they didn't believe God. Thirdly, they defied God and rebelled by not keeping the sabbath, one of the Ten Commandments. As you may realize by now, this cycle of God's people being disobedient, suffering the consequences, and then turning back to God is repeated over and over again. It looks like it's just in our nature to repeat disobedience.

1ST CHRONICLES

This is the third set of books that were divided into two books but originally written as one. The early pre-Christian translators regarded this book as things omitted or as a supplement to the books of Samuel and Kings. The information contained within this book is not simply a repeat of the previous books, but lists important information not revealed in the other books. The first part of this book provides genealogy history all the way from the first man, Adam, through king David. As genealogy is considered important to us today, it was to God as well, showing the lineage of how the Savior would eventually come. The second part of the book covers king Saul and his reign as well as his death and the reason for it. King David's reign is covered in much more detail than that of Saul.

2ND CHRONICLES

This book is a continuation of First Chronicles in that it covers in the correct, logical order points of reference and emphasis. The first nine chapters cover the reign of king Solomon and him overseeing the building and constructing of the temple at the same place where earlier, Abraham had offered his son Isaac as a sacrifice. The details of the building of the structure are provided by God, and carried out by King Solomon. Details are included here as to the kings of the tribe of Judah as well as the divisions of the kingdom in the history of Judah. The importance of this subject lies in the fact that Judah is the human tribe from which Jesus was descended.

EZRA

Most scholars believe that Ezra was the author of this book as well as Nehemiah and perhaps was the author of First and Second Chronicles. He was a descendent of Hilkia, a high priest, and Ezra was also a priest that gave his time to studying the word of God. The word of God is stressed in the life of His people that covers all parts of humanity. There are seven official documents or letters contained within this book, as well as first-person commentaries. This writing covers the return from Babylon, led by Zerubbabel. One of the main events which occurred was the rebuilding of the temple and the return of worship there. The latter part of the book covers the return from Babylon, led by Ezra.

NEHEMIAH

Nehemiah was considered a layman (not an official preacher or priest) and we learned that Ezra was a priest. This book shows how an ordinary person can have a major part in the work of God, even though that person is not considered to be operating in an official capacity or role. While some of the main parts in the book of Ezra were concerned with the rebuilding of the temple, some of the main parts of Nehemiah were concerned with the rebuilding of the walls of Jerusalem. Also covered in this writing is a great revival of the people which included the study of God's word that had been written up to that point. They had been restored and had reformed.

ESTHER

The author of this book is unknown and the book itself does not mention God's name. That does not make it any less important, for in facts, it ranks high on the list. To the Jewish people, this is one of five books called the "rolls," and it is placed with the first five books of the Bible in importance. The Jews had an opportunity to return under Cyrus but only a small number actually returned. This story is about those who did not return, but chose instead to live in Persia. They are out of the will of God. The story explains how Esther, a Jew, became the queen and married a gentile (non-Jew). It covers the ongoing conflict between Israel and the Amalekites which started back in the book of Exodus and continued throughout Israel's history. The king in this story was going to kill all of the Jewish people, but only by the divine installment of Esther as queen were the people saved. She realized that God had given her the opportunity to speak for her people and she followed through with obedience. This is not about luck or coincidence, but about God's supreme will and what happened during this time as he directed the circumstances.

For whatever things were written before were written
for our learning, that we through the patience and
comfort of the Scriptures might have hope.
- Romans 15:4

CHAPTER NINE
OF POETRY AND WISDOM

This section will cover the five books of poetry and wisdom, consisting of Job, Psalms, Proverbs, Ecclesiastes and Song of Solomon. These books are sometimes referred to as humankind's upward reach toward God. They show in a very real way that men and women can struggle with all sorts of things in life. It can be issues such as love between a man and woman, worship, forgiveness, sin, and suffering. Another item to note is that the poetry of the Hebrew language is not like the well-known classical or modern poetry that most of us are accustomed to. This poetry does not have "rhyme and meter." The Hebrew poetry has neither one of these components as they are normally structured in pairs of poetic lines known as "couplets." It is known for its parallelism or counterbalancing of ideas in phrases. Aside from the method of poetry used in these books, each one will also reveal much wisdom that can be relied upon, even in today's times.

JOB

This book was written by an unknown author but is widely accepted as the oldest book in the Bible, although there is some scholarly debate on whether it is actually the oldest book or not.

Most likely the author was an Israelite because the writer used the name "Yahweh" for God, which was the name used by them. This work was probably passed down through oral tradition and later in writing, giving the account of an ancient man that suffered with determination to be faithful to God. This is a wonderful story which shows that a person can remain faithful and true even under the worst circumstances, as Job was offered as a test to allow Satan to try to break him. Job lost everything he had including his health and his friends. His wife also turned against him, telling him to curse God. At the end of the book, we are told that due to his faithfulness, God restored him many times over what he had before. He had passed the test and remained true to God who loved him.

Job was written from the perspective of someone looking from the outside in who had knowledge of the details of what was going on behind the scenes as it played out. Many scholars think the book of Job is one of the most important books written, as it shows the perseverance of someone who is undergoing suffering from no fault of their own. These people stand up to the test and go on successfully in life. It can be related to us in today's world as having difficulties, with many believers suffering much persecution. But in the end, they do come out ahead as they are given eternal life with the creator of the universe.

This book is noted for its "parallelism," or the counterbalancing of certain ideas in phrases. To the Hebrews, wisdom included the skill in living and the power of observation in the world around them. It also included the huge capacity of human intelligence and that of applying knowledge and experience to daily life.

PSALMS

This book contains collections of what is referred to as "songs or praises" of different writers that were completed over centuries of time. It was a prayer book used in the temples and in synagogues as well. This collection of 150 different psalms makes it one of the longest books in the Bible. Some of the writings are probably the best known and quoted in the world, even to those outside of Christianity or Judaism.

There are many different types of prayers and hymns within this book. Some of them include those referred to as people's prayers to God and praise from individuals that have been saved or delivered by God. One of the most important and main themes revealed throughout the book of Psalms is related to the coming Messiah or Christ, as well as the kingdom of God. This book was put in a specific arrangement or order and was not just thrown together in some "willy-nilly" method. It has definite organization. Most of these psalms were set to music, and at the time many stringed instruments and flutes were used to accompany them. It is a wonderful collection that could be utilized as a daily reading or study by individuals that have just started their journey with the Lord and for those that have been walking many years with Him.

PROVERBS

Most of this book has been attributed to the author Solomon, known as one of the wisest humans that ever lived. It appears there are other writers who contributed, most likely men from the circle of people that were considered wise in their relationship with the Lord. This book concentrates on wisdom, with that wisdom coming directly from the knowledge received from our Creator. There are proverbs contained within this writing that give a description of almost every character in the Bible. There are also proverbs that will describe almost all of your friends and acquaintances. It defines wisdom versus folly or foolishness, with wisdom being a much better path for all of us. I personally know this because I chose a lot of folly in my life...a lot. It contains many things that are relevant to today which can help people who need direction in life, whether they be young or old.

ECCLESIASTES

The author of this book is widely accepted, due to style and content, to be Solomon, even though no writer's name is actually mentioned in the book. It can be described as a book on folly or foolishness. Much of the discussion within it shows the limits of human wisdom by itself without considering God. We think of ourselves as pretty smart creatures. After all, we figured out how the universe was created through a theory of an explosion that blew everything into existence. I think not!

This book takes into account the bigger picture of God's design and the very purpose of human existence within His realm.

The writings cover such items as the laws of nature, wisdom, and the philosophy of materialism which is living to take what you can get. We have all heard the phrase, "I have to look out for number one," putting myself first.

The wisdom shown in these writings points out the selfish nature of us human beings and our desire to make ourselves happy over everything else. Wisdom and education are two different things, as you can be educated but have limited wisdom. Again, the writings within this book are attributed to Solomon, one of the wisest human beings that has ever lived. It's well worth paying attention to.

SONG OF SOLOMON

The title in the Hebrew text is called "Solomon's song of songs," this meaning that it is a song by, for, and about Solomon. In the book of First Kings, it states that Solomon was the writer of 1,005 songs, but this book contains the best of the best. You may divide this book into four main subjects or topics, with number one being the discussion of marital relationships and how this came about or originated with God. I know this is not totally accepted by many in today's world as some people would like to do things their own way. If you look at the many examples throughout the Bible, you will find that people throughout history have always wanted to do things their way. It seldomly works out for them. I was always told you can argue with God if you want to, but He wrote it, He made it, and that's the way it is! Take it up with Him, but you don't have to argue over it with other people. The second part of this book is concerning the love of God for His nation or the people he picked and chose to bring forth the salvation of the world, Jesus. Thirdly, it's a picture reference of Jesus and the church described as the "bride of Christ." The fourth subject has to do with the relationship Christ offers with individual people and how that personal relationship is the core of what God wants with us and how our lives can be radically changed.

And you will seek Me and find Me,
when you search for Me with all your heart.
- Jeremiah 29:13

CHAPTER TEN
THE MAJOR PROPHETS

The five books which are considered the major prophets are Isaiah, Jeremiah, Lamentations, Ezekiel, and Daniel. These books were called "major" because of the amount of writings, not because they were considered more important than the "minor" prophetic books. The Old Testament prophets tended to be revealed during times of crisis and God used the prophets to provide direction and wisdom during these times. They were also used by God to remind the people of the covenants or agreements which God had promised.

The relevance of biblical prophecy is not only the information revealed about the circumstances being faced in their time or in a time to come, but also what the message reveals about the nature of God. Remember, as I said earlier, looking at the Bible in the Old Testament portion can be considered as a message about who God is. Prophecy in the Bible is part of God's "self-revelation," by which we come to know God through what He has done in the past and what He plans to do in the future.

The prophets were inspired by God and foretold of events that were to come in the near future and events that were to come further out in time. What makes the evidence that these men were speaking the words of God is that many of the prophecies have been fulfilled. And that's what makes the Bible different than any other books as people have tried to predict future events many times and have failed. But when God gives godly men direction or information about events to come, as we can find and discover in the Bible, they prove true.

ISAIAH

Many scholars today believe that Isaiah himself wrote most of this book, but they don't agree that he necessarily wrote every word. This book can be compared to the entire Bible as the book of Isaiah contains 66 chapters and the Bible contains 66 books. It has 39 chapters compared to the Old Testament having 39 books which reference the law and government of God. It contains 27 chapters compared with the New Testament having 27 books referencing grace or the salvation of God.

The first part or section of this book is related to judgment of God to come or that which has already occurred to His chosen people. Much of their disobedience by going into other kingdoms and countries has resulted in judgment which has already taken place. God is full of grace and mercy and the second portion of the book may be divided into what could be called redemption or salvation. God foretells the coming of a redemption method for humans to regain their fellowship with God through the coming savior of the world. Part of this prophecy was fulfilled when Jesus Christ was born and lived on earth. But the future portion which details His return to the world at some point in time has not yet occurred. If you look at the many prophecies or predictions that have taken place since they were written, it gives you a good idea that the rest of these prophecies will come to fruition one day. I believe that we can "bank" on it.

JEREMIAH

The author of this book is generally accepted as being Jeremiah, also known as the prophet of the "broken heart." Most of his prophecies were accomplished early on in time from when they were written and then there are others that as of yet, have not been fulfilled. Jeremiah may be described as having a "mothers' heart." He was very sensitive, but he did present a message of judgment that broke his own heart. He predicted the 70-year captivity of the people in Babylon so this made his message somewhat unpopular with his people. God is a righteous judge, even against His own people. This happened and will happen again, but He is full of mercy and gives grace towards those who will repent and turn from their ways. He will restore them, often many times more than what they had originally. This book is actually the longest in number of words than any other book in the Bible.

LAMENTATIONS

The author of this book is actually unknown, although most early Jewish traditions give credit to Jeremiah as the author. As the name implies, Lamentations is full of grief and that of "crying out." The author starts out crying over the city of

Jerusalem's misery and destruction. It gives a picture of God's anger towards His people, but it does reference God's mercy and faithfulness that will continue. In the end, it is a calling out to God for forgiveness, then turning back to Him and asking to be restored. This is a cycle that has been shown to be repeated over and over by His chosen people and by Christians today as well.

EZEKIEL

Ezekiel has been attributed as the writer of this book, and most of what is known about him is contained within it. He was a Jew, and he had been exiled to Babylon by Nebuchadnezzar. While he was there, he received a call from God to become a prophet. Ezekiel was an educated man and well versed in many topics and the knowledge he displayed indicated this. The writer details matters concerning the judgment of God against Israel which included the coming destruction of the temple. There is much symbolism and some of the language here can be better interpreted from other scriptures located in the Bible. He details God's judgment on the tribe of Judah as well as judgment against the nations. Through all of this judgment they suffered, but he also mentioned the redemption of the nation or the return to the order of God. Much of this book relates to the sovereignty of God in that He is all-knowing and all-loving, though He has the ability and will carry out judgment if needed. In the end, God is a forgiving God, a gracious God, and a loving God that shows mercy to the very people that turn from Him, but only if they come back to Him asking forgiveness and offering love would He restore them.

DANIEL

This book confirms that Daniel was the author (as well as Jesus did in the New Testament by referencing the prophet Daniel). There has been some debate over the years concerning the dating of the writing of this book, but here is a reference that would clear this up. The original Greek version of the Old Testament contains the book of Daniel which blows the theory that this was written after the fact or events that were prophesied to happen. We know more about Daniel than any of the other prophets, as his life and ministry cover around 70 years of captivity while n Babylon. God described him as "a man greatly beloved." A good bit of the prophecies were regarding the Gentile (non-Jewish) nations and much of this book concerned the Gentile people as well as the people of the nation of Israel. Some of the prophecy is shown to have been fulfilled through history, but there are yet unfulfilled prophecies to come. There is much symbolism in this book that directly relates to the nations of Babylon, Persia, Greece and Rome. It mentions a period of 70 weeks which is actually representing 490 years equivalent, and it takes us through the events of this period of time.

Oh, and let's not forget the story of Daniel being thrown into the den to be eaten and killed by the lions. King Darius had ordered Daniel to be punished this way and God protected Daniel in the middle of this "mauling by the lions" event. This shows that God has power over everything, including hungry lions!

*"The remarkable thing about fearing God is that
when you fear God you fear nothing else,
whereas if you do not fear God you fear everything else.
"Blessed is every one that feareth the Lord"* [3]

CHAPTER ELEVEN
THE MINOR PROPHETS

The minor prophet books include Hosea, Joel, Amos, Obadiah, Jonah, Micah, Nahum, Habakkuk, Zephaniah, Haggai, Zechariah, and Malachi. These books are referred to as the "minor" prophets not because they are of any less importance, but because they are smaller books than those of which are considered "major" prophets. The books of the major and minor prophets were considered to be part of the "classical prophecy" era of the Old Testament. This era began around 800 B.C., during the reign of Jeroboam II in the northern kingdom of Israel. Amos and Hosea were the earliest prophets in the north, while Micah and Isaiah were the first known classical prophets in the southern kingdom of Judah. These prophets spoke to both the kings and people and later became social and spiritual voices for the Jewish people.

HOSEA

Hosea was a prophet to the northern kingdom of Israel and his ministry lasted over a period of around 50 years. He lived long enough to see the prophecy fulfilled of the captivity of Israel. In the first part of this book, Hosea speaks about his family life and his wife, who was adulterous and could be compared to a symbolic message regarding the people of Israel in their relationship to God. The second part of the book speaks of the nation of Israel and how they became involved in the Canaanite religion. But Hosea told them to repent and to forsake the idols and return to God. He showed that the nation's main problem was they did not want to acknowledge God and they had left Him. Overall, the prophecy backs up the covenant or agreement that God had made with the nation of Israel and that He would never forget it.

JOEL

This short book is generally considered to have been written by Joel, but other than that, there is little known about him. The book is considered to be one of the earliest writings of prophets, based on the estimated time of writing. Contained within these prophecies is the literal and local plague of locusts that occurred. The future prophecy concerning "the day of the Lord" is referring to the future events of the return of Jesus Christ to the earth and setting up His kingdom. After the return of Christ to earth, it will begin the period known as the millennium or thousand-year reign of Christ as He rules over all of earth. Also mentioned is a reference to the what is called the "great tribulation," which is a period of time of many major trials and troubles on earth prior to Christ's return.

There is reference written at the time to an event, which in history for us, already occurred shortly after Jesus Christ returned to heaven after being crucified and brought back to life.

This event to come was the outpouring and work of the Holy Spirit of God that Jesus told His disciples about that would come only after He left. The Holy Spirit came to exist especially inside of believers, and this work continues to this day.

AMOS

Amos was actually a layman (not an official priest) and worked as a herdsman and gatherer of fruit. He believed that he was called of God and gave us the message that God put on his heart. Primarily, he spoke to the tribes in the northern part of the region at that time. He boldly pronounced that God was over the entire world and that all countries would answer to Him. He told them about the coming judgment of the surrounding nations for different sins against God and other people. Within this writing judgment was mentioned for the future and the nation of Israel. Some of those included visions that were described using symbolism of grasshoppers and plumb lines. Even the very nation of Israel would be punished for its rebellion against God, as they would be taken captives by the Assyrians. These visions also included the regathering of the nation of Israel and the restoration of the kingdom that is yet to come in the future.

OBADIAH

The writer of this book is attributed to Obadiah and it is the shortest book in the Old Testament, containing only 21 verses. The primary message contained in this book is still as relevant in this day that we are living as it was when it was originally given.

This book deals with pride of humans who were saying "I don't need God". God hates for man to believe that he does not need Him. Obviously, we do, as it is shown over and over again how our pride will take over in the way we live. Remember, it is a relationship with Him that He wants.

JONAH

The author, Jonah, was an actual person and the book includes a story that happened to the writer. This book has been debated by scholars and critics alike. Some have tried to persuade people that this could not possibly have happened. Jesus in the New Testament later referred to Jonah, and if Jesus mentioned him, you can depend it. After all, He is the son of God. He would know if this story was true or not. Although it is hard for some people to believe, this should help us to accept as truth other information within this book which can also be accepted as reliable and trusted. This book considers the resurrection of a person that came back amongst the living as Jonah indeed came back from within the belly of a fish. You see that Jonah was being disobedient and he paid the consequences, but in the end he was saved and God used him for His ultimate purpose. As Jonah failed to follow God the first time, the Lord did not give up on him. As God continues to not give up on the human race today, He continues to offer grace and mercy for those that will call upon His name.

MICAH

There are many Micah's that are referred to in the Bible, but this particular Micah was said to have been a Morasthite, due to him living in Moresheth-Gath. This was a village located about 20 miles southwest of Jerusalem. Many of the minor prophets addressed areas which describe or contain the tenderness or heart of God as well as the judgments.

This book may be divided into three major messages that Micah gave. The first message was addressed to all of the people. Then, the second message was mainly spoken to the leaders of Israel. This message described specific sins of the people and what they were doing. God was unhappy with the leaders having the sins of the world. The third message was from him personally, requesting for the nation of Israel to repent and return back to God. He foretold of the destruction of Israel and the fall or judgment against them as God allowed other nations to punish His people.

The coming of the Messiah "Jesus Christ" was foretold and is mentioned as the first sacrifice to allow the world to be redeemed. Also, the second coming of Christ to set up the kingdom of God on the earth is told. The first coming of Christ has already occurred and the next major event on God's calendar is the final return of Christ to set up the kingdom on earth.

NAHUM

Nahum is considered to be the author and he was an Elkoshite from the city of Elkosh and this is about all that is really known about him. The city of Nineveh was the capital of Assyria and the people had turned to God when Jonah had previously preached there. In Nahum's day they had turned against God again. Judgment is shown by God by allowing the destruction of this city due to their rebellion. God had been more than patient with the people, but his judgment was carried out completely as Assyria is no longer on the map of the world.

HABAKKUK

The author is considered to be Habakkuk and his name means "loves embrace." He was known as an embracer. He embraced his people with comfort, letting them know that God is in control. Habakkuk has a problem understanding what's going on with God because there are people that are more sinful than his people, but yet they are not being punished. What he discovers is that God is working and He is very much aware of the problems. He is preparing judgment for the nations that have come against Him. It was still hard for the prophet to understand because it wasn't the way he would do it. I think we all do that today in many cases because we don't believe that God has it under control and we have our own ideas for solutions. I know I do that. But if we believe in God, we should remain faithful and have patience, realizing that He is in control and will handle the issues at hand in His timing.

ZEPHANIAH

The writer of this book identified himself through his family lineage going back to his great-great-grandfather, who was Hezekiah, the king of Judah. One of the main themes of this book was for him to advise Judah of God's coming judgment. The destruction came by the Babylonians after they had destroyed Assyria and brought that power to an end. This writing references the judgment of Judah and Jerusalem. Also covered in the prophecy is the coming judgment of all nations as well as the new kingdom being established on earth still to come.

HAGGAI

Haggai is attributed as the author of this book, one of the shortest books in the Old Testament but still very important. He was a prophet that urged the people, which had been under Babylonian captivity, to rebuild the temple since Solomon's temple had been destroyed. Cyrus, the king of Persia, had offered the Jewish people the opportunity to return to Jerusalem and rebuild the temple. This rebuilding and reconstruction of the temple was the most important thing to this prophet. He actually scolded the people for delaying the rebuilding, but he also encouraged and helped them along. Haggai was very upfront as to the supreme authority of God and was thankful for allowing him to give the message of claiming the word of the Lord.

ZACHARIAH

Zachariah was a prophet, but he was also a member of a priestly family or lineage and is considered the author of the entire book. One of the main subjects of this book is to point out the failures of the people of Judah, as well as encourage them in the rebuilding of the temple. This writer gave more Messianic prophecies (those of the coming of Christ) than any of the other minor prophets. He gave warning through the ten visions he had received. Contained within these visions were prophecies concerning the second coming of Christ to be fulfilled in the future. Encouragement from this prophet is a major subject of the book, emphasizing that God will restore His kingdom on earth one day.

MALACHI

The author of this book is considered by most scholars to be Malachi, whose name means "my messenger." Malachi was considered to be the last prophet of the Old Testament times, but there are those that disagree and say that Joel was the last. He gave messages to the people concerning the love of God for the nation of Israel. He also rebuked the priest and the people for their sins. The book also has prophecy of the coming messenger relating to John the Baptist who would announce or proclaim the Messiah. Also mentioned is the prophecy concerning the return of Christ after the tribulation period on the earth.

This concludes the brief surveys of the books of the Old Testament and I trust that they are not too lengthy to bog anyone down. I only wanted to give some highlights of truths found in these very important books and it is not exhaustive by any means. I hope and trust that these surveys offer encouragement to seek for yourself the truth and to explore the many good references out there that are available for Bible study. Remember, we are taking steps!

So shall my word be that goes forth from my mouth.
It shall not return to me void, but it shall
accomplish what I please, and it shall prosper
in the thing for which are sent it.
- Isiah 55:11

Chapter Twelve
The Good News

There was a period of time after the last writing of the Old Testament had been completed which was silent or nothing was recorded. After a period of around 350 years, the beginning of the New Testament started with the ministry of Jesus Christ.

In the following five chapters (12-16), we will be covering those divisions or selections of books in the New Testament portion of the Bible. As we continue through our "step-taking," these divisions are pertaining to the 27 books of the New Testament which for the most part were originally written in Greek.

The first four books of the New Testament are called the Gospels, and they include Matthew, Mark, Luke, and John. These New Testament writers were people who were eyewitnesses. They walked with Christ and wrote down the things about Him and the things He said. Consequently, these books may be considered "biographical" in their nature. The word "gospel" comes from some words that mean "good letters, good words, good news" as the gospel writers wrote of the good news of Christ. These gospel accounts were about the son of God coming to earth and His ministry throughout the time He was here.

MATTHEW

The gospel books begin with the book of Matthew, describing Jesus' genealogy and where He came through human lineage or bloodline. This gives us a reference in a clear path from how Jesus was born. Many people would ask why this is important and what difference does it make as to what bloodline He came through? The difference is that it matters because in the Old Testament, prophecy foretells how from the beginning to the last book in the Old Testament that a Savior would come. These prophecies revealed how Christ would come and it told whose descendants He would have. That's why it's important as the New Testament shows and demonstrates the truth revealed earlier in the Old Testament and how Christ would be born in human form. The book of Matthew reveals the life of Jesus, who He was, and some of what He did while on the earth. Most scholars believe that Matthew himself authored this book. He was a former tax collector and was one of the 12 apostles of Christ. This book covers facts about Jesus from His genealogy to his birth along with His teaching, healing, and other miracles that He performed. Matthew wanted to help people understand that Jesus was indeed the Messiah, the Savior of the world. Also included are some references about the end times of the world. This is not a long book, but the information it holds is of upmost importance to the reader in order to provide some of the written story concerning Jesus Christ. Also included are some of the most important occurrences within this book as it is related to Jesus's execution and crucifixion, His death, and then His resurrection back to life.

MARK

This is the second book of the four gospels and the authorship is attributed by most scholars to Mark, also known as John Mark. John was his Jewish name and Mark was Latin surname. The book of Mark seems to emphasize more about what Jesus did and not so much what He said. The style is short and to the point.

John the Baptist is introduced early on and announces the coming Savior, Jesus. It is revealed here that God recognized and authorized Jesus as His son and that He would offer deliverance for humankind. There are many different healings of people through the miracles of Christ that are mentioned throughout this text. Along with the miracles relating to human beings, there are also some that pertain to Christ's control over the laws of nature. One of these miracles was pertaining to Him walking on water, defying the very laws of gravity and not sinking below the surface.

On the spiritual side of things, there are several instances of Christ dealing with control over demons or evil forces that tried to present themselves against God at the time. There are also some parables included that are basically human or earthly stories that have a heavenly meaning. Overall, there are many miscellaneous teachings throughout this text that apply to different important subjects related to His teachings. And of course, the all-important view that Mark offers on the death, burial, and resurrection of Jesus Christ is phenomenal.

LUKE

Luke has been recognized as being the author of this book and he also has been attributed to writing the book of Acts as well. Luke was most likely a gentile (non-Jew) and was actually a physician by trade or education. The writer was obviously educated and had a firm handle on the language of the day. Some of the material in this book is to help strengthen the faith of believers and to answer attacks that were presented by unbelievers. He wanted to show to everyone that the gospel was the good news and the teaching of Christ was for gentiles as well as for the Jewish people and the entire world.

JOHN

The final book of the gospels is John. This was written by the" apostle" John and was also noted within this scripture as the "disciple whom Jesus loved." This book is different from the other three gospels as his account about Jesus goes in a different direction. The main point throughout this book is that Christ was and will always be "all God" in the human form and He provides clear authority. He speaks of who Jesus is and His mission along with going even further back in time to where Jesus was before the world was even created. Jesus was revealed as being with God and at the same time was God, a major point in describing who Jesus was. He states in the message "for God, so loved the world that He gave his one and only son that whoever believes in Him shall not perish, but have eternal life." This statement of truth is the absolute foundational point of the gospel messages of these books.

"We can understand the attributes of God in other ways, but we can only understand the Father's heart in the Cross of Christ." [4]

CHAPTER THIRTEEN
HISTORY - THE CHURCH

This chapter will cover the book of Acts which details the beginning history of the Christian church. Acts is the only biblical book that covers the history of the church, which began shortly after Jesus Christ ascended to heaven. This, of course, was after His death, burial and resurrection that was detailed in the earlier books of the gospels. The church grew and expanded out from Jerusalem throughout the land of the Mediterranean world. All of this happened while the early Christians were persecuted in many ways, especially from the Roman empire. There were literally many people who were punished and even died due to their proclaiming the work of Christ. Still, the church grew and later expanded throughout the entire world and now has become the largest religion in the world.

ACTS

The fifth book of the New Testament is known as "Acts of the Apostles" or simply "Acts." Acts covers the beginning and history of the early church. The word "church" here does it mean a denomination or group, but the body of believers or followers of Christ. As I stated earlier, this book is commonly accepted to have been written by Luke, one of the apostles who also wrote the book of Luke. This book serves as a bridge from the gospel writings and the introduction of the church. It gives direction as to what and how the church was to operate. These guidelines remain as vital instruction for the church today.

The historical account of Christian origins is a major part of this book, as it tells of the founding of the church, the spread of the gospel, and the start of congregations or evangelistic movements. This account refers to the beginning and the spread of the church as a direct result of the risen Christ, and the Holy Spirit which came after Jesus departed, which continues to work today.

There were many things that the early church was dealing with such as the pagan beliefs and even the legalism of the Jewish traditions. This book addresses those issues (and more) as it helps to explain the principles and doctrines which are contained within this holy book. It also details the successes of Christianity in spite of the heavy persecution it was under from the Roman empire as well as other forces. Other points covered are the historical detail of the times and locations of the church.

One important person mentioned in the book of Acts is Paul (Roman name) also known as Saul (Jewish name). Paul is considered to be one of the most impactful men of the Bible, as his writings counted by number of words is attributed to around 25% of the New Testament. This is second place to the number one writer, Luke. Paul was actually a Roman citizen because he was born in the city of Tarsus under Roman rule. He was also Jewish and a Pharisee or leader of the Jewish church, very devout in his heritage and discipline. His father was also a Pharisee and Paul started out persecuting Christians.

Paul later had a direct encounter with Jesus Christ that changed his life forever and he became an apostle to the gentile people of the world. He became a true missionary, taking the gospel message throughout Europe and Asia Minor. He would work miracles in God's name and became an important church leader. He probably did more to spread Christianity than any other one person, other than Christ Himself. There are many books that have been written about Paul's life for you to explore and to learn more about this apostle. I highly recommend that you search this out later.

It is kind of odd that God would use a person that would start out being so much against Him. But this is the way God works in many cases, not in the "normal" sense of the word, but He uses people and circumstances that go against the natural order or sense of being. That's what makes him God.

"The Bible is the only Book that gives us any indication of the true nature of sin, and where it came from." [5]

CHAPTER FOURTEEN
LETTERS OR EPISTLES TO
THE CHURCHES

The group of 13 books, which were actually letters or epistles written to the churches by the apostle Paul, are Romans, 1st & 2nd Corinthians, Galatians, Ephesians, Philippians, Colossians, and 1st & 2nd Thessalonians. The other four books of 1st & 2nd Timothy, Titus, and Philemon were addressed to church leaders at that time. All of these letters are still quite relevant to today's times as churches still continue to struggle with following the correct doctrines and the handling of internal affairs within the body of believers.

ROMANS

This book was written to the church in Rome and conveys the message of the gospel: God has a plan of salvation and righteousness for all who come to Him regardless of their race, standing in life, or how they were raised. This includes Jewish and gentile (non-Jews) and it is explained through Romans, highlighting the message of how to be reborn or become a child of God. All of this is related to restoring or converting to fellowship with God (what He desires) and how to become closer. It also explains a great deal about the confusion that was going on between the Jews and what they had understood in their life under the law of Judaism. This would reveal the freedom that Christ brought to them. Quite simply, salvation is explained in this book to demonstrate that believers can be freed from sin and from the law and death through a relationship with Christ Jesus in God's sovereign plan.

1ST CORINTHIANS

This letter was written to the church which was located in the city of Corinth. The city was a fairly large area with a lot of busy activity going on, much of it not in a very good way. It was considered by many to be "the center of sin" within the Roman Empire at that time.

Now the church was beginning and starting out with a good bit of confusion as to some of the basic doctrines of what Jesus had brought forth. These problems, of course, spilled over into the church. People who lived there brought into the church some of the thinking and ideas of what was happening in the city. Paul tries to help them out with correction. There were divisions in the church and he also addressed some of the moral and ethical problems. He lays out the foundation of the church, beginning with the importance of the crucifixion of Christ and clarifies this point. Along with this, he clarifies the work of the Holy Spirit within the body of believers.

They didn't really understand church discipline and how to handle things that were going on within the church that weren't right. Paul gives instructions to help with issues such as the problems that married people face. These issues were all going on with everyday people and especially the leaders who worked in the church. A good bit of this particular letter is devoted to giving or outlining corrections and the clarification of issues that were misguided at the time. Keep in mind that these instructions are also relevant in today's time, not just for those who lived back then.

2ND CORINTHIANS

Paul went on to explain in this letter to the church in Corinth that God was a God of comfort. This comfort he was presenting comes as an assistant and sustainer of people. He further outlines in this writing the importance of giving by believers to those causes within and outside of the church. As part of the comfort that he covered, the work of the Holy Spirit within the believers is explained in more detail. By the way, the Holy Spirit is also known as "the comforter.". A good portion of these two letters could be considered "problem-solving "letters that addressed issues and truths that needed to be explained in more detail. This was and is needed in order to help people understand the correct interpretation of the scripture being written. Again, these instructions are very important in our lives today.

GALATIANS

Most scholars believe that this letter was addressed to the churches that were either located in north central Asia Minor, or the southern area of the Roman province of Galatia. They are not certain, but scholars believe these two areas were where the churches were located. A good many of the new Christians were located around this area, especially the people of Jewish descent. They still held on to some of the practices of the Old Testament and had a hard time getting away from what they'd grown up with. This is understandable, as what they had known all their lives had been disrupted and they didn't really quite understand this "Christianity" completely.

Paul first established that he had authority in proclaiming these words because of his personal encounter with Jesus Christ. He counted himself as an "apostle" due to having had this contact directly with Christ himself. His life was radically changed from a persecutor of those who believed in Christ to a preacher of the gospel of Christ.

He goes on in this writing to explain foundational doctrine, along with the truth of the cause and purpose of Christ and what He brought to the human race. He wanted them to know and understand what Christ came for and what He wanted the church to be...more importantly, what He wants us to be.

EPHESIANS

This letter was written to the church in Ephesus, but it was circulated to other churches as well. Paul was said to have been imprisoned while he wrote this letter, as he was with the three other books - Philippians, Colossians and Philemon.

He did not write them regarding specific things they may be doing wrong, but he gives an overview of issues that the readers can understand. These include what God had done in the past, and some of His plans for the future. This relates back to God's eternal purpose and the goals of the body of believers known as "the church." He tells of God's remarkable way of revealing that He is wise and has purpose with everything.

Paul states that one of the reasons God seeks a relationship with human beings is that He wants us to share the life that He has given us with others. This enables us to enjoy and to have purpose in our life with connection to the body of believers. He also covers topics such as gifts that He gave to the church to help them with reaching people. This book can serve as a reminder for people to help them understand the heavenly goal. The effect of what happens to people as believers is provided to empower them to go forward in this world.

PHILIPPIANS

This book also was written while Paul was imprisoned and is known as one of the "prison epistles." Paul seems to emphasize the word "joy" in this book and much of it is based on the fact that joy can be found, regardless of your circumstances. After all, he was in prison still talking about joy. He wanted to encourage the people in the city of Philippi to continue striving forward, even though they were undergoing persecution. Things were not easy and he wanted them to be strong in the Lord and to continue their mission.

The book is rich and filled with giving people instructions on how to live and how to be encouraged in the middle of trials or problems. The importance of looking forward as we step into the future without wallowing in our past failures is one important instruction given.

One of my favorite verses in the Bible comes from Philippians Chapter 3, verse 13. In part it states, "but one thing I do, forgetting those things which are behind and reaching forward to those things which are ahead." You see, if we can just keep our eyes on the things that are ahead and put those things behind us that are in the past, we can press forward towards whatever lies ahead!

COLOSSIANS

This book was written to the church that was located in the city of Colosse, hence the name Colossians. Apparently, this church was in danger of some of the so-called modern thinking that was going on. At the time there were a lot of philosophies circulating around. There were certain forms of mysticism in the area and Paul tries to address the errors along these lines in order to assist the early Christians. With that, he offered an explanation on some topics of the truth concerning the church and Christian living. Paul emphasized that Christian living is the theme and Christ is the center, not Christ-plus-something or Christ-minus-something.

These issues that were addressed in this letter are still a concern to the modern day church. Some of today's churches have slowly allowed some acceptance or drawing in by combining ideas that really don't have a place within the church. The books we have in our possession today were written, in part, to clarify subjects in order to keep people on the proper path. But as we can see, people will vary for a "little here and a little there" and they will put in a "little bit of this" and a "little bit of mix it up" and this makes for a pleasant thing for people to listen to or experience. But, it's not the truth. Jesus said "I am the truth." He didn't say "me-plus-something or me-minus-something." As hardheaded people, we can have real difficulty dealing with something presented as "one way."

1ST THESSALONIANS

Thessalonica was a Roman colony and also an important hub within the dominion of the Roman Empire. This letter was written by Paul and considered one of his earliest letters written while on his second missionary journey. It was an open letter sent to a group, even though some of the writing seems like he may have been directing it towards one individual.

One of the themes seems to be directed to help confirm to young converts to Christianity the basic truth of the gospel message. Also, it was written to help them understand the merits of holy living and to comfort them with the promise of Christ's return. This book, as well as other books in the Bible, were not written in an "essay style" and because of this, it can sometimes appear to be somewhat "rambling" in subject matter.

2ND THESSALONIANS

This book may be considered as a continuing "sequel" to the first Thessalonians book as it continues discussions about misunderstandings. For example, the time when Christ would return and the need for all of us to live in anticipation of that return is explained. He tells us not to get tired of the pressures and not to get tired of living good and right while living on earth. His message was "don't be weary, carry on, and continue in the faith." The topics cover the Christian's attitude towards the return of Christ as well as rewards that will be forthcoming and what can be expected in the death of our human body. A large amount of information is packed into these short writings.

The following four letters were considered "pastoral" epistles which were written by Paul and addressed directly to church leaders:

1ST TIMOTHY

This letter was written to a young pastor named Timothy who had several things happening in his church. There were a lot of false teachings and issues within the church that needed to be addressed. Some of them related to the proper handling of problems as well as the qualifications of leaders within the body of the church. Again, this word "church" is referring to the group of believers. It is not referring to some denomination like Baptist, Methodist or Catholic.

What we see in these passages of this book are areas that are still going on today as problems within many churches. As with many of these letters that Paul had written, they were providing instruction as to the order and steps that God desires for His church to operate under.

2ND TIMOTHY

Paul in this letter, which is which is said to have been his last, knew he was reaching the end of his life and, he had fought the good fight. He wanted to see Timothy again as he was very fond of him. Timothy was like a son to Paul and he went on to say that there was "no one else like Timothy." Paul was writing this as the church was turning away from the truth and teaching things that weren't part of the gospel message. This mixture of philosophies had crept in and corrupted the very word of God.

Paul was encouraging Timothy to persevere, go forward, and to remain strong and faithful, telling Timothy to guard the gospel and protect it in every way he could. Finally, he encouraged him to keep preaching and to keep telling others of the good news of what Christ had done for the world. These were his instructions, and he added that it may be necessary to suffer persecution. He was encouraged to be strong and continue with the message.

TITUS

This letter was directed to Titus, who was a gentile, not a Jew. The book may be considered a type of operating manual or measuring stick for the New Testament church. It is supposed to be an orderly organization and it definitely should practice sound doctrine. The church should be pure and ready to do the work for the calling of Christ. He speaks of the coming or return of Christ to the earth and how we should be looking forward to this. He gives instructions for the operation of church as an outreach, not only preaching the gospel of Christ, but that of doing good works in the community. This is not necessary to become a Christian, but as a follower of Christ they should have a desire to be of service in the local church. In other words, doing good works shows evidence of the Spirit of God in a person's life. He also lists the responsibilities and qualifications of the elders of church. One other thing that Paul stresses is that the church is to preach of God's grace, the favor of getting what you don't deserve that He constantly shows to people.

PHILEMON

This letter contains only one chapter written to Philemon, and most likely was completed while Paul was in prison. Philemon was a slave owner and one of his slaves, Onesimus, had apparently stolen from him and ran away. This crime under Roman law was punishable by death. He had met Paul earlier through his ministry and had actually become a Christian. Onesimus was going to return to his master and Paul was asking that he be accepted as a brother in Christ.

One of the main points of this letter is to reveal that Christ loved us and pleaded our case to God. It is considered the first illustration of "substitution" as God provided Christ to be our substitution and take on our sins in order for us to be forgiven.

Also, Paul teaches brotherly love. If we are in Christ, then we are brothers and sisters and we should practice love towards one another. Many of the letters Paul wrote were addressed to individuals and they were considered personal. They had a different meaning than some of the letters that were written to general congregations.

Give instruction to a wise man, and he will be still wiser;
Teach a just man, and he will increase in learning.
- Proverbs 9:9

Chapter Fifteen
To The People

The eight books which were written as "general letters" to large congregations of people are Hebrews, James, 1st & 2nd Peter, 1st, 2nd, 3rd John, and Jude. These books provide information to help us know more about who God is and verifies what we are reading truly comes from Him. They also provide information that can help us understand how we should live our lives while still walking around on the earth. These truths are all important because people are watching Christians and they are attentive to the actions of folks who call themselves Christians.

Trust in the Lord with all your heart,
And lean not on your own understanding;
In all your ways acknowledge Him,
And He shall direct your paths.
- Proverbs 3:5,6

Hebrews

There are some arguments as to the author of this book. Some attribute it to Paul and others disagree. This may be considered a book of a "better way," meaning throughout all of this, Jesus Christ was and is "the better way." It further describes that Christ is superior to all of the prophets, to angels, and far superior to Moses. Up until the time of this writing, Moses had been considered one of the greatest Hebrews that ever lived.

The book of Hebrews explains the priesthood of Jesus and that He was truly "the pathway" offered for the entire world to come to God. The Old Testament covenants had been fulfilled by Christ. He became the better and more secure way for all people. There is an explanation of the duties benefits, and responsibilities of being a Christian.

In Hebrews, Christ is shown to be much better than any animal sacrifice previously offered since He was presented by God as the "ultimate sinless sacrifice." This paid the sin debt that the human race had to pay in order to regain that relationship back with God. The writer gives some of the dangers of people doubting and taking on philosophies that are not contained within scripture. He also speaks of the danger of not listening and departing from the faith, leaving it or abandoning what they have been enlightened to. The sacrifice of Christ was the only sacrifice that could pay the penalty for humankind and their sin. Temporary sacrifices had been required in the Old Testament in the way of animals or blood being offered. Jesus became the ultimate sacrifice as the sinless, blameless human form as part of God and equal with God offered as our substitute. This brought life back to humankind and gave us the only way to restore fellowship with our Creator.

JAMES

This book is considered to be one of, if not the earliest, books of the New Testament which was written by James. The writer explains the major differences between faith and works. Faith may be called the "root" of salvation and works are the "fruit" of salvation. In other words, faith is what helps to bring salvation into us and works are the results of that salvation.

This book explains that God will certainly test our faith with trials, but He will never tempt us. Tempt and test are very different words. God will test us according to the word of the scripture. He will test us by the way of our attitude, our actions, and by what comes from our tongue. We also have trials that can test our faith which are indeed part of life.

Some of our testing can be applied to our willingness to do good works. We do not do good works to get God, but because we have Him already in our hearts and soul, we want to do good for Him. James also mentions the return of Christ when He will one day come back and take His people with Him. The subject of the power of prayer by Christians is also emphasized. Oh, what power there is in the prayers of the people that belong to Him! God hears our prayers and wants that communication from us. In order to have that link we must first have a relationship with Him.

1ST PETER

This letter was attributed to Peter, who was one of the apostles of Christ. Many believe that Peter may have had some help with writing this since he was not as educated as some of the others. Peter has been called an ignorant fisherman due to his occupation. But I think that anyone who spent the amount of time with Jesus like he did, should not be referred to as "ignorant." Peter grew in his walk with Christ and learned about himself and who Christ really was. You can see this through his writings as he became totally committed to Christ. Peter told about the suffering of Christ and of believers, Because Christ suffered, so will Christians.

He does speak some about future events regarding the second coming of Christ to this earth and tells of the horrible things that will go on beforehand. The coming catastrophes that transpire will produce holiness and it will have an effect on the forwarding of the gospel message around the world. He also gives some guidance on Christian conduct and how they are to behave in the home and church.

2ND PETER

This letter is understood to have been written shortly after the 1st Peter. This was the last letter from him as it came before he was martyred (killed) for his faith. And Peter wanted to give assurance that the full knowledge of God is the main foundation on which the character of a Christian is built. He wanted to show the authority of the Scriptures, where they came from, and how they came about. We also tried to do some of that in the first step of this book that you are now reading.

He talked about the "turning away" by people due to the influences of false teachers and teaching. The history of what God's agenda was in the past, the present, and in the future world is presented. And finally, he gives direction to believers for them to lead a holy life, reminding them of the importance of the return of Christ back to earth one day.

1ST JOHN

The author of this letter is John, the son of Zebedee, an apostle of Jesus that had walked with Him. It was written primarily to believers and it was circulated to churches that were in existence at the time. There are several points that John makes here in this letter, one of them being the fellowship of believers with one another. He also gives encouragement so that our joy may be full and that we don't need to continue living a sinful life. One of the other primary points he makes is that you can know without a doubt that you have eternal life if you believe in the son of God, Jesus Christ.

God is described as being light that shines and illuminates the true nature of people. The writer reveals that God is love and believers should walk in love and should be known for their love for one another. I think we sometimes forget this, and that's about all I'll say to that right now.

The other important part of this book explains that God provides life in death even after a person's physical body passes away. God provides life as an eternal form, never ending. Overall, this is an encouraging book and gives explanation to some important doctrines.

2ND JOHN

This letter was also written by the apostle John, and apparently was written specifically to a lady or particular woman in the church. It was also circulated and many churches read this letter for instruction in the church. He emphasized the importance of love being within the fundamentals of truth. There were a lot of untruths (lies) at the time due to false teachers and other accepted false doctrines of the day. John wanted to emphasize that the people bringing these false doctrines were not supposed to be welcomed or helped. People that rejected the truth of Christ were not true believers. He was looking forward to an upcoming visit with the person/church to whom he had written.

3RD JOHN

This letter has some similarities to the previous book of 2 John, as it is personal and continues the theme of truth. In the 2nd John letter, the idea revealed is that truth is worth standing up for, and in this third letter, it is that truth is worth working for. He states in verse 4 that he had "no greater joy than to hear that my children walk in truth." His "children" here refers to the young converts and leaders of the church at the time.

JUDE

This book was written by the brother of James, known as Jude. Both were actually half-brothers of Jesus Christ. He started this letter giving assurance to believers, and then changes the theme to what is known as apostasy. Apostasy is someone who once professed to be a Christian and then totally walks away and rejects it all.

He gives a background concerning this turning away from the truth, or rejection, or distortion of it. He references the Old Testament examples of Israel wandering in the desert and being destroyed. He even speaks about the fallen angels of heaven and their turning away and rejecting God.

There are many references concerning those people that would distort and try to destroy the gospel message. Believers should remember the truth, and they should know the word of God and have it written on their hearts. Instruction was also offered as to what believers should be doing in the coming times of rampant distortion of the truth. Today, more than any other time in history, the distortions and lies concerning the truth of God seem to be flourishing.

I will instruct you and teach you in the way you should go;
I will guide you with My eye.
- Psalms 32:8

CHAPTER SIXTEEN
THE APOCALYPSE

This book of Revelation is the final book in the New Testament and the last book of the Bible. It was written by John the apostle, and believed to have been written while he had been banned and placed in exile on the island of Patmos. This was a result of him being persecuted for his role in spreading Christianity. At the time persecution was becoming quite intense against Christianity's beginnings.

REVELATION

The book itself reveals that John was "taken up in the spirit" and allowed to see the things which are recorded in this writing. He was told to write down what he saw and send this to the seven churches in Asia at that time. This was a supernatural experience as he was taken up, not physically in his body, but his spirit was allowed to receive the visions recorded here.

Revelation, or the Apocalypse (meaning unveiling or revealing as scholars generally prefer to refer to it as), is very descriptive and prophetic, dealing with future events. This book is sometimes seen as a confusing book, especially for people who do not understand or have knowledge of biblical contents. It does describe many areas utilizing symbolism and allegory in the out-line for surrounding biblical events. The book itself gives inter-pretations for many of the items that are described within it. But there are some that may not be totally agreed upon by scholars of the Bible. Keep in mind that although there are differences of opinions on some of the elements or interpretation within this book, these differences do not affect any major doctrine of the en-tirety of the Bible. So, in following that thought, I'm not going to delve into those issues. I don't want to make this too complicated and confusing for you, so I'm going to try to keep it simple. If you take steps in trying to understand the Bible, Revelation can actually be fairly easy to comprehend.

It is the only book in the New Testament that deals mostly with prophecy as 17 books in the Old Testament deal with future events. The book may be broken down into three sections with chapter one referring to past events, chapter two and three cur-rent events, and chapter four through 22 describing events to come.

The first chapter or section of Revelation has to do with the person of Jesus Christ, describing what He had done, how He has come for humankind, and then the description of His glori-fied body. The second section or chapter two and three are deal-ing with the position of Jesus Christ with the church in the world as divided into seven churches. They are actual churches, but can also accurately describe some church types operating in today's world. The third section, chapter four through 22 describes the coming agenda of Jesus Christ and the things that are going to happen when Christ returns to earth. There are many references within the Bible of several prophecies that have already been accurately fulfilled. So many have already occurred that it should help us all anticipate the rest of the prophecies being fulfilled. God revealed a glimpse into these future events to help us prepare and not fear, but instead look forward to His plan ahead.

As we have seen in these somewhat brief descriptions of these 27 books of the New Testament there are viewpoints from different writers expressed in these books. The subject matter varies between the books and as a whole. Looking at these books can be seen as miniature steps in the understanding of the gospel message.

The New Testament is about the gospel. It is the good news and shows the redemption story that God provided for us and our relationship with Him restored. In the beginning, in the garden, shows how God walked with humans. He had fellowship, He was personal, unlike any other religion on the earth. We too can have this relationship with the Creator of the universe and the creator of humans. I know this may sound so ridiculous to many people, but it doesn't change the fact that it is possible for us to have that relationship...if we take those steps toward God.

As I stated earlier, these brief descriptions you have just read over all 66 books of the Bible are my own way of giving a look into each book. There are many commentaries and study guides that drill deeper into the meanings and all of the parts of these books that are well beyond what I wanted to explain. I didn't want to overwhelm you, but I wanted to give you a taste from my perspective of some of the highlights of these books. They are all open for you to study and look at the "meaty" parts of these books that I didn't even touch on. I strongly encourage this.

The Bible is unlike any other book as the information can be considered letters from God and they are revealed to us by the truth in them. We begin by taking steps towards God. These steps never end, as people have studied and studied the Scriptures their entire lives and everything can't be fully exposed due to the supernatural method of revelation to humankind.

There are many translations out there, some good, some not so good. You have to be careful because just like anything out there, there are some phonies that are corrupt in their translations. Some of them are not even really "true translations," but are only paraphrases that go under the title of translations, but they are not. Some versions of the Bible are translated by people that have no training or experience, but only translate the word of God to fit a particular religion. The bottom line is that everyone who claims to be a Bible translator doesn't mean they are.

The best versions are produced by people who are well-educated and considered expert scholars in their fields of Hebrew, Greek and Aramaic, languages, and dialect. And some of these scholars have been studying these languages their entire lives. You must be careful do your homework and make sure that whatever translation you're using is an accurate and verifiable translation of God's word. Again, you have to do your homework and make sure that what you are getting is reliable.

The Bible itself explains that the scripture is given to us as an inspiration from God. It is for our good, and for us to be able to learn about Him and to understand and grow in our relationship with Him. That's what makes these writings so special because they come from our heavenly Creator.

> *"Jesus Christ reveals, not an embarrassed God,*
> *not a confused God, not a God who stands apart*
> *from the problems, but One who stands in the*
> *thick of the whole thing with man."* [6]

PART THREE:
THE THIRD STEP -
THE SOLUTION

IT'S RIGHT IN FRONT OF US, FOR ALL TO SEE

[1]In the beginning was the Word, and the Word was with God, and the Word was God. He was in the beginning with God. All things were made through Him, and without Him nothing was made that was made. In Him was life, and the life was the light of men.
- John 1:1-4

WE HAVE NOW ARRIVED AT THE THIRD STEP IN THIS PROCESS

It may be seen as the final step, but only as it applies to this book. This final step will build upon the established steps we have taken earlier.

As we ponder what we have taken in at this point, it can also be a beginning step. This will hopefully continue our step-taking towards the truth of our Maker. We have just taken a closer look at the individual books of the Bible and some of what they reveal. Many books are available which have been written about the individual books, as well as particular verses in the Bible. These writings offer much more detail and cover much more of the material contained within them. I want to encourage you to explore, research, and delve deeper into what these remarkable books contain. We will begin to go forward into explaining this journey and the remarkable stories weaved into the word of God. And remember this: "It's right in front of us, for all to see. It was created just for you and me!"

CHAPTER SEVENTEEN
LAYING THE GROUNDWORK

In this chapter, I will lay the groundwork for the rest of this part of the book. There is so much more information within these writings that I am omitting, but I'm not trying to cut you short. My goal is to give you a picture that will go along with the purposes of this book.

The Bible remains the best-selling book of all time throughout the world. I think that is important to at least consider and take a look at what has been done over time to keep these writings available to us. Also, a topic relating to history for us to consider is the archaeological evidence that has been discovered which proves many of the events and occasions brought out by scripture to be true. They continue to find evidence to this day of the reliability of what had been revealed early on in these writings. These discoveries actually validate occurrences which otherwise may be doubted or looked upon as having no merit.

The Bible presents many instances where prophecy or events which were foretold have come true and been fulfilled. In the prediction of the coming Messiah, Jesus Christ alone, there are over 200 references of prophecy that were fulfilled during His short ministry on earth.

One of the most important pieces of evidence to me is not considered logical, scientific or archeological, but it is evidence nonetheless. That is in the area of transformed lives and people from generations back that have been radically changed and brought into further knowledge through this great book. There are literally millions of people around the world in different cultures and countries that have been affected by the revelations contained within the Bible. It can't be explained by some laboratory method or some equation related to science. In fact, it can't be explained in the normal realm of things at all. You see, the letters that are recorded within this book contain a link back to the One that created us. We can argue over the details and some of the points, but the bottom line is that these letters are supernaturally brought to us as "letters from God."

Here is a short recap of where we are on our "step-taking." We first looked at where this information and writing we call the Bible came from, how it was preserved, and how it got into our hands today. We examined the reliability and accuracy of the documents which provided the sources for these writings to be passed on to us. We looked at the actual number of scriptures and documented textual evidence which is available today. These messages were preserved throughout history even though there were attempts by certain people to destroy them. Over thousands of years these writings were preserved in many ways not equaled by any other ancient writings found on the earth.

The second step we have taken is a brief description of each book of the Bible. Remember, I have only provided snippets of information with these brief surveys. The Bible offers insight and enlightenment which could not have been revealed by luck or coincidence, but obviously had an outside influence much greater than us. I only covered some of the highlights I felt were important for you to see, and my hope is that it has sparked your interest into digging deeper and looking for yourself the revealed truth within the Bible.

My daughter and I were talking one day and she told me that to her, the Bible can be overwhelming or hard to understand sometimes. I get that, but there are some important things that go along with reading and understanding the word of God that are not part of any other literature you may read. As God offers us direction in our lives, He also provides enlightenment or understanding to His words which are written down.

The Bible states in 1 Corinthians 2:14 that the natural man does not receive the things of the Spirit of God, for they are foolishness to him; nor can he know them, because they are spiritually discerned. Natural men do not understand the spiritual things of God.

"Natural" here means a person that has not accepted these truths, and not accepted the Spirit of God into their lives. They don't have the ability to understand the words that are in written in this book. That's where it begins, the first step. That is where it starts once a person receives the Spirit of God into their heart and lives. You could compare it to having a car that has no fuel in it and goes nowhere because it has to have the fuel. Well, the Spirit of God is the fuel.

The Bible has been studied by some people their entire lives and still continues to open up more and more in the way of understanding until they pass from this life to the next. Again, this is a book like no other book that has been compiled in the world.

In this last section of the book, I will try to explain the thread that runs through this entire book of books. In other words, what is it about, what does all this mean, what is in it for me, and just what is going on here? I will attempt to offer this third step that will hopefully tie everything together in a way which will enable you to take steps toward God. Hopefully you will better understand what God has done for the entire human race.

Having said all of this, I would like to now zoom out a little bit from this collection of 66 books to take a look at the bigger picture. Following our previous outlines, we will begin with the Old Testament books and continue with points or highlights, and then will cover the New Testament, providing insight there. This will include an overview or a broader picture of what is included in this great collection of books.

"God created man to be master of the life in the earth and sea and sky, and the reason he is not is because he took the law into his own hands, and became master of himself, but of nothing else." [7]

Chapter Eighteen
Beginning The Journey

As we have seen in our survey of the books of the Bible, God gave to humans the story of where it all began. In the first book and first verse of the bible, God reveals the account of creation of the universe and of the planet earth.

In the beginning God created
the heavens and the earth.
- Genesis 1:1

God took steps in the creation of everything day by day for six days and the final step that He took was the creation of human beings. I want us to take a brief step back and look at this account of creation in comparison to the modern-day scientific approach that has for the most part been widely accepted. There are many scientists who believe that the stars, solar system, planets (including earth), and moons traveling around planets somehow came into being from this major explosion or "big bang" that blew everything into existence. In the beginning all of these early planets just banged around with rocks and material. Some of this material stuck to other pieces and some of it shaved off some of the pieces and formed these little balls in space called planets. Now all of these things work together and that's the way it is today.

They can't really explain where it all originated from or why the bang happened or where all this original material came from, but nonetheless, they claim that it just happened randomly. The evidence of a creator? This idea of a God that created everything? Why, that's ridiculous!

Much of what we believe is derived from what we have been taught, whether through school, parents, TV, friends, etc. I propose that it's a little different than that and we are here due to what some modern-day folks call "intelligent design" or what I call "God-created." You see, there is way too much coincidence for all of this to have happened for me to believe it just developed itself out of some random falling together.

The planet we call home or earth is placed exactly where it needs to be as related to the distance from the sun; not too cold, not too hot, just right. Oh yeah, the gravity we have is just the right amount for us too, keeping us from spinning off into space and keeping our weight where it needs to be! Scientists haven't quite figured this gravity thing out either. The tilt of the earth on its axis of 23.5° is one of those other little "funny things" that happened a long way back in this "self-creating" planet. Guess what? Without this tilt we wouldn't have the seasons of the year and you can bet that might have a huge impact on the overall grand operation of things. It's just really amazing, isn't it?

Let's talk about our moon that just "happens" to be the right size and in the exact place (not too far, not too close) to help provide tides (with help of that item called gravity) that are imperative for the health of the oceans and the planet. This gravity also helps control the speed at which the earth rotates, another serious factor that could cause problems. Without the moon, our days could be six to 12 hours long and we could have years one 1,000 days long.

Look at all the different animals which have developed or adapted to different climates, locations, or habitats necessary to their survival. Notice I said "adapted," not evolved, as there are no animals in existence evolving into some other animal – none. All were created differently and distinctly with design in mind.

Then, take the human being, a vastly different animal. The human body and mind are so complex it can't be figured out completely. We consider things or have intellect which allows us to have a reasoning of time like the future or future events to come. Humans are made up of around 100 trillion cells, with the brain alone having about 100 billion nerve cells.

Take just one part of the human anatomy, the eyeball. It is about the size of ping-pong ball and has over two million moving parts. And we have two of them! So let me get that straight. Humans just came out of some random goo and created ourselves on our own, decided to put in or build ourselves two of these things called eyeballs. Never mind the rest of our bodies, like the heart, lungs, bladder, and most importantly the machine that controls all of called the brain. The odds of this all happening has to be way, way, way, way out there don't you think?

All of this was placed together at precisely the right points in time including the planets, the sun, the moon, the animals, the plants and even human beings had to be designed or built by something or someone. But who is this designer? I once had a discussion with someone in my family as we were riding along in my vehicle on a stretch of highway through the bountiful forest of Georgia. He had a background of designing and building, so he had a good idea of the steps need to make things. I asked him to look around and see the beauty of the world and all that was in it. I asked him, "Do you think it just popped into existence?" He said it must have because men are the builders of things, I don't think there was any design, it just happened. I then asked him, "Do you know that the Bible says God created us in His image, meaning that we have some of His features, like designing and building formed in us?" Only silence came afterward from him; no answer, no comeback, and no response, just silence.

I have a great friend whose name is Lamar. We recently talked about how people and their pride prevent them from just accepting the truth of God. If we think or believe in God, then that's like saying we are weak and not smart enough to figure everything out which makes us look not so bright. That's where the pride comes in, by not realizing the limits of our intelligence and wanting to appear as though we have it all together. We just don't want to give in and admit the fact that we are not as smart as we think we are. It doesn't matter how many letters we have after our name.

To sum this up, for me it takes much more imagination and stretching our minds to think for one single minute that all of creation just happened by coincidence. The Bible is a book which was supernaturally given to us as a record of not only God's creation, but of who God is and of His sovereignty and desire for a relationship with us. As God, He is more than capable of doing everything that has been done, including making the earth and us. To think that the God of the universe who created everything wants a relationship with humans is amazing to say the least. Why would God who has this kind of power want a relationship with us lowly humans? It is an amazing wonder and mystery that He does, but that is the basis for everything we have in front of us as evidence from our Creator.

Life is so much more important than how we can make money, build houses, drive nice cars, and have everything we want in the material realm including our own happiness. Life is short, and our years are numbered. We will not live in this physical body forever. But our very soul, which makes us different from any other animal on the earth, will live and go on into eternity. That's the way we were created.

Ok, let's get back to the story as it was. God gave us the order of creation of things and included in this creation was human beings. The result in recorded history tells us that humans were created in God's image. In other words, we have some of God's features. The earth was created as a perfect place in that it held everything needed. God instructed the first humans to take anything in the garden or on the earth for their use. But He gave them one rule. That one rule was not to eat of one particular fruit on a tree.

God told them if they were to eat of that forbidden fruit, it would open them up and expose them to the knowledge of good and evil. God did not want humans to partake of this. He did not want them to disobey His one and only rule. Remember that God only wants good for us. Even in these beginnings He warned us for our benefit. But along came a tempter in the form of Satan. We learn from scripture later on that Satan was actually an angel of God that became overwhelmed with his own pride and thought he could be equal with God. He was removed from heaven and took some of the other angels along with him and decided to go it on his own.

This tempter, Satan, approached Eve and put doubts in her mind by asking her, did God really mean what He said, did He really mean not to eat of that tree? Finally, he convinced her that maybe that's not really what God said after all, and through her doubting, she decided to try this forbidden fruit. Afterwards, she convinced Adam to do the same thing with this tree because it didn't harm her, so it must be OK. Adam made up his own mind and willingly disobeyed God doing exactly what he wanted to do. Eve didn't make him do anything, so Adam doesn't get a pass by blaming it on Eve. Enough said.

God has given them everything on this perfect planet for their good and wants nothing but good for them, walking and talking with them in the garden, fellowshipping with them. He gave them that one direction for their own good not to do. In this creation story for the beginning of mankind, you have the human race with everything they needed, but they decided for themselves to get a little more even though they had direct instruction not to do it. That's kind of like us today. When we get everything that we need, we always want to get a little more. That's how we are as humans.

After mankind had chosen this path, things were different on earth. The human race would experience many things to their detriment. Even as humans took the path that God knew they would, God was already at work. He already had knowledge of a plan to offer a path back to fellowship with Him.

You can read about the children of Adam and Eve as some of the earliest examples of the downfall of mankind, as we see in the story of Cain killing his own brother Abel. This needless killing took place because of man's anger and man's pride. You see, they both were to bring sacrifices to God and Cain brought sacrifices that were from his garden, but no animal sacrifice as his brother Abel had brought. Surely, they both understood what was required of them, but Cain did not do what he was supposed to. When Cain saw that Abel and his sacrifice brought happiness to God and his did not, he became mad at his brother with enough anger to kill him. The relationship that God had with humankind early on was, at this point, separated due to man's disobedience, but God still required certain things to be done His way.

As the story of humankind continues, we come to an area where the people of the earth had turned from God in the account of Noah. At this point in time God looked upon the people and the Bible says:

*That the wickedness of man was great in the
earth, and that every intent of the thoughts of his
heart was only evil continually.*
- Genesis 6:5

But God identified Noah as a man that walked with God, so He instructed Noah to build an ark as God was going to destroy the earth with a flood. He gave specific instructions on how to build it with the dimensions and design details. He also told Noah that He was going to make an agreement or a covenant with him. He was instructed to bring a certain number of animals of the earth and his family into this ark and they would be saved from the flood.

As we can see in this early story of the history of humankind, man invariably turned from God, but God in His mercy provides a way forward. The people in Noah's day began to trust in themselves and to think highly of themselves and saw no need to worship God. Even in this early account, God was making a path forward because through the lineage of Noah, He would later choose His people, and would direct the coming of the Savior of the world.

Not long after the account of the flood on the earth, the people built what was known as the "tower of Babel." The descendants of Noah wanted to create something that would show their own greatness rather than giving credit to God. As a result of this building of the tower, the languages of people were split up and people from that point in time were known by different languages of the earth. In this part of history, mankind takes its own direction and learns the hard way, that it's really not the best way.

Later, there was a man named Abraham who was called of God to be a leader. He made a covenant with Abraham regarding his people. There is a great deal in the story of Abraham that is contained within scripture, but there are a few things I would like to mention here about Abraham.

God had told Abraham to leave his home and travel to a land that God would show him. He further gave assurance that a great nation would come about from him and that He would bless him and make his name great. He would be provided with rich land and be the leader of the nation.

They left and traveled to a land called Canaan. While they were there the weather turned and ushered in a harsh famine so Abraham and his wife Sarah traveled south toward Egypt. Once there, Abraham tells the Egyptians that his wife is his sister because he feared the Pharaoh would kill him in order to take her. The Pharaoh wanted to marry her, but God sent a plague upon Egypt, thus stopping the marriage. Afterwards Sarah was restored to Abraham and they were told to leave Egypt. God had other plans for them.

Abraham had been told by God that he would make him fruitful and that he would be the father of many nations. Well, Abraham became older and his wife could no longer conceive a child, so they decided to help out with the process of having children. Sarah offered Abraham her handmaid Hagar to bear a child for therm. Of course this was not God's plan and was not with

His permission. That's just like us humans as we want to give God a hand with His plans because after all, we are pretty smart!

Abraham was assured by God that Sarah would bear his child, and Sarah was visited by what was believed to be angels telling her that she would indeed bear a child even in her old age. Sarah did become pregnant and they had a son named Isaac. God later instructed Abraham to take his son Isaac and offer him as a sacrifice. Abraham, being the obedient follower of God, did exactly as God told him and took his only son up to Mount Moriah to offer him as a sacrifice. His faithfulness and his obedience were rewarded in that God provided an animal sacrifice to take the place of Isaac who was about to be offered to God. This wonderful story that took place with Abraham and his only son was a precursor to the coming sacrifice that would be offered to all of humanity at a much later time. God would provide His only son, Jesus, for the perfect and only sacrifice that would be offered in our place to provide that relationship with our Maker. As we know through the genealogy of Abraham, the nation of Israel, as God's chosen people, would come as direct descendants of him. The wonderful stories of Abraham's descendants continue on with one of his great-grandchildren, Joseph, who was sold by his brothers and taken to Egypt. The nation of Israel later became slaves in the country of Egypt, and God raises up Moses to eventually lead his people out of slavery. How God delivers His people over and over is an important subject by itself which reveals many different events that have occurred throughout history. Before the people were released from being held as slaves under Egypt, there are different plagues recorded that affected

Egypt and came upon their land. Each one of these plagues represented God's ultimate control of the forces of nature.

Moses was also given the ten commandments by God after having led the people from captivity and then on to the promised land. Along the way, God had come to Moses in the form of a burning bush and appeared to him with directions. Although Moses had led the people for many years, he, along with some of the people of that nation. were not allowed to enter into this promised land.

We read that Joshua was the one who received the leadership role after the death of Moses and was allowed to lead the people into the promised land. The nation of Israel was ruled by different judges for periods of time. Later on, the nation of Israel set in place its first king, Saul, and then after him was King David. Many people have heard or know the story of David and his encounter with the slaying of the giant Goliath." As a small shepherd boy, God had his eye on him and used him to defeat the people that were against the nation of Israel.

This same David later on committed adultery with a woman that was married. As a result, the woman became pregnant and bore his child, which later died before he was named. To cover it all up, David had the woman's husband killed in battle. Even this great servant of God, that the Bible says, "was a man after God's own heart" was still a human being with a tendency to do things his own way.

Solomon, the son of David, became one of the greatest kings to ever rule over the people of Israel. He was also known as one of the wisest men to have ever lived. Israel later became divided kingdoms which became known as Israel to the north and Judah in the south. These regions had different kings ruling for periods of time leading up until the nation of Israel's northern part being conquered by Assyria. Then Judah, the southern half, was captured by Babylon. Many of the people of Israel returned to a demolished land and intended to rebuild the temple. This was in part due to their desire to usher in the new covenant which the prophets had told them about.

There are stories throughout the Old Testament that even include talking donkeys. Another event recorded is of Jonah being tossed overboard from a ship at sea and being swallowed up by a giant fish. He remained inside the belly of this fish for three days before he came out alive and well. I don't want to forget the story about Shadrach, Meshach, and Abednego, an account of these men being thrown into a fiery furnace to be destroyed. They were saved when an appearance of some other "being" showed up with them in the fire. All of them came through the fire without even the smell of smoke on their clothes.

Throughout the books of the Bible there are many stories that may seem strange or confusing, but if you read through the books in the proper context, these stories come alive and have a richer, deeper meaning. Throughout these letters it shows over and over again God's mercy on people that are bound to make mistakes. God is rich in mercy and forgiveness for those who will call upon Him and turn back to the one that from the beginning wanted that relationship.

As we saw in our brief studies of the books of the Old Testament, the prophets foretold of many events which later occurred. Many of these predictions have occurred later in time. Also, there are those which were revealed that have not yet happened. These truths can be depended on as another method in verifying the reliability of the writings which were given to us supernaturally by God.

I want to again encourage you to explore for yourself this vast book of knowledge. Within it the stories that are told are about real people that were involved throughout history in documenting events which were important and still relevant to today. You can see that people have a tendency to behave somewhat selfishly and with disobedience to authority repeated throughout history. The Bible says there's no "new thing" under the sun. In other words, it's all been done before by somebody at a different time and a different place.

One of the important threads woven throughout these records is that God used regular people, not necessarily the "royalty" type. Many of these examples were simple everyday folks. What makes some of them stand out is the fact that even though they had issues (like all of us), they had an overall desire to please and serve God, regardless of their calling. As we saw in Genesis, the relationship with God to humans was very personal and He only wanted good for them. The plans that God has for us and what we do can be totally different, but these books reveal that God will work it out for His purpose, regardless.

Hopefully, all of this will pique your interest so that you will consider the source and importance to which it could be in your life. In many of these stories, you may ask why God did all of these things that seem so strange to us. I suggest because we do not know God's heart. I believe that in many of these cases they defied the very standards or laws of physics and nature that God ordained. It shows that God is in control and can use any of these miracles to show that He has the ability to change or alter the very forces He put in place. Only He could do that. He chose to use the small, the humble, and the seemingly unimportant for His glory and purpose. Much of what God does can't be explained in human terms because we don't have the mind of God. We are extremely small in comparison to His wisdom and power.

"The vital relationship which the Christian has to the Bible is not that he worships the letter, but that the Holy Spirit makes the words of the Bible spirit and life to him." [8]

CHAPTER NINETEEN
HE CAME FOR YOU AND ME

As we zoom out and look at the New Testament portion of the Bible, we can see that Old Testament scriptures are quite often referenced, giving authority and relevance to the connection between the old and the new.

As I stated earlier, the New Testament books which are considered the "gospels or Good News" are the first four books of the New Testament. They primarily describe Jesus Christ and His brief life while on the earth. The rest of the New Testament books may be thought of as the working of the Holy Spirit of God. This also involves the action of the Spirit to this day on the earth, as He fills believers in their lives and hearts with His very power.

Let us take this step here on our continuing walk towards God as we take in the New Testament perspective and the important letters to us regarding the Savior. We have stretched from the beginning of creation of the universe, earth, and humans to the rich stories that were told throughout history of God's interaction with humans. This all came to a point around 2,000 years ago when God chose His plan to restore a bridge back to Him through the ultimate sacrifice of His son. Jesus Christ was born and lived as a child in the form of a human being in order to bring about His purpose on earth. The story is so simple, but yet many people find it complicated, hard to understand or they don't approve of the methodology or even the race of the chosen people. We now have all of these other beliefs which are mostly based on how we can work our way into an eventual utopia. Remember, Christianity is not based on what we do, but on what God has already done for us. And the relationship with us that He offers is unlike any other religion in the world.

The first four books of the New Testament include a great deal of information about Jesus Christ. Matthew gives us information surrounding the birth of Christ and how that miracle came about through a woman, Mary, a virgin. It also reveals a portion of the genealogy and family history which traces Christ's human family through people that God had favor with and chose to deliver this ultimate sacrifice for humankind.

Written within these books are stories of Jesus as a child and some of the astonishing things He did, amazing those around Him at the time. It can be verified that many of the details surrounding His birth were mentioned and prophesied in over 100 places in the Old Testament books. God said that sin came into the world through man, which was Adam, and that salvation or redemption will come to the world through a man. Jesus was and is that man. Even though He was human, He was all God and came as the salvation offered to the world.

This is how God directed the events and I'm not about to explain why God did what He did, but I do know that I can trust and believe in what He did. He took steps through his childhood and had no sin in Him as He was God dwelling in the human flesh. I'm sure as a child He played with other children and explored things as He was learning and growing in His human capacity. This growing and step-taking was accomplished while having the supernatural attributes of God.

His earthly father, Joseph, was a carpenter and Jesus grew up around that trade, making and building things. Can you imagine working alongside of Him in the shop? I enjoy working with wood as a hobby and I know the frustration that comes with trying to get pieces to fit just right. I'm sure Jesus had some of the same difficulties working with wood, especially since their tools were much more primitive than what we have today. I can't help but think that some of his work probably turned out as perfect as He was.

It is recorded that Jesus's earthly parents, Mary and Joseph traveled to Jerusalem every year during a Jewish holiday known as the "Feast of the Passover." The Bible states that He was 12 years old on one occasion and stayed behind in Jerusalem. When His parents returned to get Him, they found Him in the temple, sitting amongst the teachers talking with them, listening, and asking questions. All of the people who heard Him were astonished at His understanding and knowledge. This 12-year-old boy somehow had knowledge that was beyond understanding.

Jesus's arrival to begin His ministry as an adult was announced to the world by His cousin, John. He was introduced as the Lamb of God (or sacrifice), as John knew of Jesus and who He was. Jesus caused quite a stir among the people, going to the hurt, the needy, or the people that no one else wanted to serve. He knew they needed that relationship with Him, just like the people of today. And many of those folks did not appreciate or think of Him as godly, especially since some of them wanted everyone to think they were godly. Jesus came for people who recognized they needed the relationship that only He offered.

Many of the so-called religious leaders of that time discounted Jesus and refused to acknowledge Him as God and in fact, thought it was blasphemy that He equated Himself to God. They were high and mighty thinking folks and thought they could look down their noses at all of the little people because they felt like they had it all together. They thought this because they were supposedly keeping all of the laws and commandments, so they looked at themselves as having arrived.

When Jesus's ministry began, He called his disciples to go with Him and be the closest people in His inner circle. He went to them with His message and told them to follow Him. He did not beg or plead with them, He just simply said, "follow me." When He came to earth, he relied solely on God and was directed by God's will to perform the things according to His direction. The Jewish people were expecting and hoping for the Messiah to set up His kingdom, and punish all of those who needed punishing. Jesus came as a child, born not in a castle, but in an animal manger. They did not understand what was happening in front of them.

Why would God come to earth and be born and raised to some ordinary people, living in a human body working with His hands as a craft maker? This simple life was offered because God wanted all the glory to come to Him and not from some worldly stature, which in the end doesn't really mean anything. This story today gets a lot of people confused and I can understand that because if we look at the way things are in the world, this story just doesn't make sense. After all, somebody that's a king ought to have all of the attributes of a king, but He certainly didn't. What the people didn't understand at the time was that Jesus would come and serve as take on the sin of the world and become the ultimate sacrifice. He would not establish His kingdom on earth…yet. That is a future event as Jesus Christ will come back, and will set up His kingdom on earth. But this will be done like everything else, in the steps and order that God chooses to get there.

It is understandable for some people to have missed the evidence of who was in front of them. The stories that are revealed include Jesus ministering to people and changing their lives forever. Not just in the physical form, as He did heal many ailments, but He demonstrated His power over the human issue of our separation from God.

Jesus gave many messages and sometimes spoke in stories to people in what's called "parables" or stories with meaning of purpose. The stories He told were directed to the people of that time. They could relate to and understand what He meant. Jesus even raised people from the dead and brought them back to life, a miracle which could only be done supernaturally, not by any other means. Jesus traveled throughout the region with the message that included the fact that He was God in the flesh and that His time was coming. The "time" referred to His death and sacrifice He would pay on the cross.

His own disciple, Peter, was told by Jesus that he would deny Him and that he would claim not to even know Jesus. This event is recorded in these letters, Later, Peter watched from a distance as they led Jesus away after He was arrested. The Roman officials brought Jesus before them due to the demands of the religious leaders and people of that day. They saw Jesus as a blasphemer and His claim to be equal with God must be dealt with. When they brought Him before the people on the charges, they also brought another man, Barabbas, before them who had been charged with much more vicious crimes. The Romans gave the people a choice of who they should let go and be freed. The people chose Barabbas to be freed and Jesus to be crucified.

The Roman authorities symbolically and literally washed their hands of this act to show no blame or responsibility for the punishment to be carried out as the people chose. The sentence was decreed and Jesus was led away to be tormented, tortured, and ultimately was nailed to a wooden cross to die. The crowds went wild with excitement as their hatred for this man became clearer and clearer. Jesus suffered beatings and thrashings before He was nailed to the wooden beams to hang by His own body until His death. As He hung on the cross, the soldiers gambled for the one piece of clothing that Jesus owned that was of any value. On each side of Jesus were two men who had been sentenced to death and crucifixion as well. One of the men denied who Jesus was. The other man accepted Christ, saying that he knew that He (Jesus) was indeed the son of God. Jesus told this one that He would see him in paradise. In other words, he was forgiven and through his belief in Jesus as the son of God, he would inherit eternal life.

The Bible records that one of the soldiers took a spear and punctured the side of Jesus. Blood and water poured forth out of His beaten body. Jesus asked forgiveness for what they had done to Him. He stated from the cross, "it is finished." It had been done as God permitted and He passed into a physical death of His body. He was removed from the cross later and taken to a tomb that He would be buried in. It was secured by a large stone that was placed in front of the entrance to prevent anyone from stealing his body. Also, guards were placed in front of this area to make sure that no one tried to remove Him.

The ability to comprehend why or how Jesus could be killed if He was indeed the son of God, was not understood by most everyone there at the time, including His disciples. But that's not where the story ends, it really continues after Christ was sacrificed as that perfect lamb of God and His human body was put to death.

On the third day following His death, there were two women who had gone to the place of his burial to anoint his body with oil and to wrap Him with cloth in a common burial method. When they arrived at the tomb they found the stone had been rolled away. and angels appeared to them announcing that Jesus had arisen and left the tomb. He left the tomb where He was placed to be held and kept in burial. Death had been defeated. He allowed death to come to the physical body, but it wasn't permanent; it was temporary. He offers that same eternal life to us.

As the women returned back to town to tell the disciples that Jesus's body was gone, a man spoke to them. This man was Jesus. They realized who He was and with excitement they returned with the news of what had happened to them. Meanwhile, the disciples gathered together in a room, shaking their heads in disappointment that Jesus had been killed. All of the things that happened left them feeling like they had been wrongly persuaded. They had been walking with Jesus, saw the miracles He performed and lives that were changed. Their hope and trust grew along the way, only to see everything come to an end. It was utter disappointment for them.

Jesus himself later appeared to the disciples and confirmed that He was indeed alive. One of the disciples, Thomas, who wasn't present at the time, after being told of Jesus's appearance, said that he would only believe if he could touch the scars in His hand and side. Jesus appeared to them again while Thomas was present and told him to feel the scars on His human body. Thomas then proclaimed that it was indeed Jesus, the resurrected son of God. Jesus stayed on the earth for another forty days, teaching and preaching, and witnessing to many people that He was indeed alive. The records reveal that He appeared to all of the apostles and over 500 believers at one time.

During this time, Jesus met with the disciples and gave them instructions to go into the world and tell the good news of what had happened, teaching and preaching in His name. He told them that He was going to send a comforter, or His Spirit, after He departed and returned back to heaven. They later witnessed Jesus being taken up into the sky as Jesus left in what is recorded as the "ascension of Christ." The angels which were present at that time told them that Jesus would return again one day. They were told not to lose heart but to take comfort in that promise, and to go back to Jerusalem to await the coming of the Holy Spirit.

I want to say a few words about the resurrection of Jesus Christ and relay some personal observations as to what I believe make the case for Christ even stronger. Jesus was placed in a tomb by Roman soldiers and a large stone was rolled in front of the opening. Guards were placed there as well to prevent anyone from trying to recover His body and then proclaiming that He had disappeared. The Romans were very serious about their duties, and there was no way they were going to allow anyone to come and take Him. To think that somehow someone convinced these soldiers to allow them to take His body is ridiculous. If there had been any way for someone to retrieve the body to show the world and prove that He was still dead, they would have gone to any expense to do so. They could not put a dead body on display and if they could have, it would have been recorded in history. This would have ended Christianity before it got started. None of the apostles would have given their lives to be put to death like they did for a dead Savior.

*I am the way, the truth, and the life. No one comes
to the Father except through Me.*
- John 14:6

CHAPTER TWENTY
THE SPIRIT OF GOD

As we continue along in this New Testament portion, I will offer my explanation as to the third part of God that operates on the earth in the form of the Holy Spirit. God is a three-dimensional being in that He is God, He is the Son, and He is the Holy Spirit. I have heard of others compare this action of God to an egg which has three parts that make up the whole egg: it has a shell, a yolk, and the clear or white part. Altogether these form the whole unit of the egg. Not a great comparison, but it may give you the idea.

Anyway, God as the creator of everything utilizes three distinct operating forces which work together as a whole and have existed throughout eternity. As we have seen previously, human beings are created in the image of God and human beings just happen to operate with three main parts as well. First, we have a physical body. Secondly, this physical body holds our eternal spirit or soul, which makes us different from any other creature on the planet. Thirdly, we also have a mind or an operating mechanism within us that keeps everything working within this physical body.

During Old Testament times, the Holy Spirit came to earth and worked in people and in circumstances, but generally did not remain here on earth. After fulfilling His time on earth and before He returned to heaven, Jesus had stated that He must depart, but He would send someone else to carry on the work here on earth. This someone else was the Holy Spirit, also referred to as the "comforter." This was the Holy Spirit of God that would come to earth and work in the daily lives of convicting people of this truth, and then living and residing inside of people.

What is known as the day of Pentecost is celebrated by Christians, and occurred about ten days after Christ had ascended back to heaven. This event happened at an important festival time on the Jewish calendar, which was known as "Shavuot." It was a celebration of harvest time, or of first fruits on the first harvest. The timing was of no coincidence to God, as Pentecost became the first coming of His Spirit in the beginning of harvest season for believers throughout the world. This appearing and arrival of the Spirit became a powerful event which is still evident to this day, as the work of the Spirit of God continues.

The beginning of the "church" or you could say, Christianity, really took off at this time with the arrival of this power. The Bible records this supernatural event as believers gathered together from different parts of the world and spoke different languages or dialects. The description given is that they all heard a sound like a rushing mighty wind, and it filled the whole building while they were there. There were also appearances of divided tongues that appeared like a fire that was above their heads.

The people there were filled with the Holy Spirit and they began to speak in other languages. It goes on to say they heard everything spoken in their own language. There was one voice, but all of the people with different languages understood everything in their own language. Some of the people that were nearby thought they had been drinking some alcoholic wine as they were all acting strangely. Peter told them that they were not drunk, but that this occurrence was what had been prophesied by the prophet Joel in the Old Testament. This supernatural occurrence records that about 3,000 people believed and accepted the Spirit of God in their lives. The beginning of the Christian church had arrived.

The Old Testament method for a relationship with God was through a temple building where people would come to worship God and bring a sacrifice to be offered by the priest for forgiveness and worship. After Jesus left, the temple became the human body and the soul of humans is where God in the form of the Holy Spirit can now reside. The old method involved going into the temple to worship God. Today, we are the temple, and we allow God to enter and live inside of us. Pretty amazing isn't it?

This residing of the Holy Spirit within a human being begins when a person calls out to God, and in faith ask for forgiveness of their sins. A person must ask that God come into their heart, into their soul and fill their life with His presence. In the book of John, Chapter 3, scripture describes a man named Nicodemus. He was a Pharisee and a member of the Sanhedrin, which were the primary leaders and teachers to the Jewish people at that time. He went to see Jesus at night because he didn't want others to know he was visiting Jesus because they might condemn him. He realized that Jesus was of God. Jesus told him that a person must be born again or he cannot see the kingdom of God. Nicodemus asked Jesus, "how can a man be born when he's old; how does he enter back into his mother's womb?" Jesus then described the process of having a human birth and being born of water. But then the birth that occurs in your soul, or by the Holy Spirit, comes to you and resides in you. Jesus again repeated, "you must be born again."

This "born-again" phrase is also used today using the terminology of "saved or salvation," which all mean the same thing. It is a rejuvenation, or a rebirth that happens within the human soul and spirit, and it is a life- changing event. I would suggest reading John chapter 3, verses one through 17 for some additional details on the indwelling of the Spirit in a person's life.

After the event of Pentecost, the church was started, and disciples were called to go about and provide witness to the things they had seen and heard. The church was now empowered through the work of the Holy Spirit. The lives of the people were forever changed. The Bible reveals that the church grew daily as more and more followers and believers of Christ accepted this gift of the Spirit in their lives.

One of the most important stories of the beginning of the church came not long after the event of Pentecost. There was a man named Saul, who was a Pharisee. The name Saul was his given Hebrew name as he was Jewish by birth, and since he was also a Roman citizen, he had been given a Roman name of Paul. He was a leader within the Jewish church and he swore that he was going to wipe out this new movement of followers of this so-called Messiah. He had letters from the high priest which authorized him to arrest any followers of Jesus in the city of Damascus. Now, while taking the road to Damascus, Saul and his company of people were struck down by a blinding light. Saul heard a voice say "why do you persecute me?" and asked who was speaking. The reply came that "I am Jesus who you are persecuting." He told Saul to get up and travel into the city, and he would be told what to do next.

Saul had been blinded and could not see, so they led him to the city of Damascus to a man named Judas, and for three days Saul did not eat or drink. Jesus had also appeared to a disciple named Ananias, and He told him to go to Saul. Ananias was afraid because he had heard about how dangerous Saul was to the Christians. Jesus reminded him that Saul had been chosen to deliver the gospel message to the gentiles and to the kings and people of Israel and the entire world regardless of their background. Ananias found Saul praying for help and he laid his hands on Saul, telling him that Jesus had sent him to restore his sight, and that he would be filled with the Holy Spirit.

Saul's sight was restored and he then rose up, and was baptized in the name of the Holy Spirit. He stayed there with the disciples in Damascus for three days and after this conversion began using his Roman name, Paul. He had been a killer of those who had faith of Christ. He had arrested and put to death any that were part of this new church. But after this encounter, he showed that Christ came for *everyone* on earth, including both Jewish and gentile people.

Since Paul had seen the risen Christ in this vision, he was considered an apostle of Jesus. He was a man that had been educated in the Jewish culture and language, and had been brought up in the city of Tarsus. This allowed him to become familiar with the Greek language and culture. All of this helped him to bring out the Old Testament text and connect it with the New Testament when it was being written.

Paul became one of the writers who produced around 25% of the volume of words in the New Testament books. He became a staunch defender of the faith, and went on to explain some of the proper directions and order. Many of these writings were addressed to particular churches at the time and were vital instruction which provided for the correct interpretation and growth of the church. They are still very much relevant to today's church.

In the book of Corinthians, we find the record where Paul tells of being whipped by the Jews five times and then he was beaten with rods. He was stoned, struck with rocks, shipwrecked three times, and he had been in the water for a night and a day. Paul was repeatedly put in prison in order to prevent him from spreading and taking this message throughout the world. He was familiar with the people's anger towards Christianity and hate of Jesus Christ as he traveled around the country proclaiming the message. He continued to have a heart dedicated for the churches and people in them, helping establish the truth of this message.

The recordings in the New Testament are filled with different accounts of some of the apostles being arrested. There are accounts of miracles that were performed through these apostles as they worked to establish the church. The Bible records that the number of new disciples was increasing, and even that a large number of Jewish priests had become believers. The disciples and apostles traveled around the areas preaching and proclaiming the truth of what had happened and the church grew. There was much to be explained in this "new relationship" which was offered through Christ by making the Holy Spirit available to people.

The Old Testament was filled with laws and directions for people to live by. But this New Testament church where people were first called Christians was different in that the importance was on the relationship -- the relationship of people to God through Christ and the Holy Spirit. These people were used to treating people better that were of so-called "high importance," giving them the best seats in the house. Christ turned that around and said that all of us, even the lowliest, should be in the best seats. He said we give so that we get. We die in order to live. These were huge contradictions of thinking during that time, and even in today's time.

So, what are some of the things that happened as the New Testament church spread throughout the area? There were apostles and disciples who were killed and murdered because of their taking this new Gospel to the public. Several missionary journeys are recorded leaving records of events which occurred through their travels and involvement with the churches of that day. Much of the work throughout the New Testament documentation reveals the working of the Holy Spirit within the body of believers and the power that came with it.

The book of Revelation is the final book in the New Testament and it primarily deals with prophecy of future events. The apostle, John while exiled on the island of Patmos, was taken up in spirit and given a view of future events to take place on earth. He was told to write it down and that's what we have in this book. There are a lot of people who get confused in this book and it can be confusing, especially to those that may have little or no biblical knowledge. The best way to interpret this book is to look at what the Bible says about the things within this writing. I had an old preacher tell me a long time ago that the best way to interpret the Bible is to look at the Bible. That's because in most cases, the reference or interpretation of the terms or uses of them, can be located within the pages of the Bible. Many answers to questions are lined up with other scripture throughout the Bible. Don't be afraid to examine this book, as the importance of a look at what will happen in the future of the earth is an interesting topic. Keep in mind the great number of foretold prophecies that have come to be.

A short zoom-out view of this part of the New Testament includes the fact that God reveals a period of time when the message of Christ will be preached around the world. Theologians love this book as it has been dissected and looked at from many different viewpoints. Since it contains future events, the discussion takes on many different forms. The basics are that there will come a time when God alters the operation of His church on earth, and many believe that He will remove all of the believers at a given point in time. These radical changes will happen and we do not know when, and the Bible says that no one will know, not even the angels in heaven.

There will be a period of major disruptions on the earth, including catastrophes, famines, major deadly weather events, the greatest earthquake that humans have ever experienced, and problems of all sorts. But after that time of trouble, Jesus will return back to earth and bring people that have already gone on to be with Him in spirit form. Jesus will set up His kingdom on earth and reign for 1000 years. Later there will be a new heaven and a new earth created, and the old earth will be destroyed. There will be a judgment day coming for every person that has ever lived and will ever live on this planet. We will all appear before a judgment seat of God. For the people who have accepted Christ, there should be no worries of this coming time. The hope and truth which is in them has made them free and will protect them, taking them through this time in His hands.

But if the Spirit of Him who raised Jesus from the dead dwells in you, He who raised Christ from the dead will also give life to your mortal bodies through His Spirit who dwells in you.
\- Romans 8:11

Chapter Twenty-One
Do We Hear the Calling?

If you recall in the first part of this book, I stated that this step-taking process could be of importance to believers as well as non-believers alike. A believer is a person that has trusted in Jesus Christ, asked for forgiveness, and has received the gift of the Holy Spirit into their heart. I also said that people could be somewhere in between these two groups, and hopefully this book would offer something for those folks as well.

That calling, or voice speaking to us through the Holy Spirit, can and will come to all of us at different points in our lives, regardless of our spiritual condition. For a believer in Christ, that calling or whisper will come to you in the form of the Spirit speaking to you, urging, offering guidance and direction in your life. Jesus repeatedly said to people, "Follow me" and to follow Him requires that you listen to Him. God attracts or nudges us with the Holy Spirit, that same part of God that convicts or draws men and women to Him.

If you have never trusted in Christ, there may have been moments of time when you felt a desire that you couldn't explain. That is how God works in humans as He draws them to him by this convicting Spirit. As humans we are not robots who are pushed around by God, as we have a choice or free will that allows us to tune out this calling. We can subdue it, we can run from it, and we can get away from it, but in the end, we will have to decide whether we want it or not. The choice for us is whether we believe it or not and whether we accept the gift that is offered to us or not. That is every person's choice at some point in their life.

I believe that God comes to us at different occasions in our lives, and I also believe that He really never gives up on us. But, I also believe that we can reach a point after turning Him down over and over that the convicting call could subside or even cease. The Bible is clear that God is not willing that any should perish, but that anyone can call upon Him and be re-born.

Christianity is the only religion that gives each human being a purpose and offers the ability to maintain a relationship to the creator of the universe. Most all other religions are based on what you do, what you can do, how many times you pray, where you pray, how many doors you knock on, or how many things that you can do good so you may be treated fairly after death. Some people even spend their lives inside of caves or buildings worshiping God, but living isolated lives. They really do not have much affect on the world as they are not living amongst the world, but they are working hard. These are what's called "works-based" religions and they are based on what you do or on how hard you work. And if you work really hard and do enough, you may work your way into heaven. But you never really know if you've done enough or if you're going to be part of those chosen few that get to enter heaven.

True Christianity is not based on what you do, but on what God has done for you. It's a matter of accepting this, taking hold of this truth, and making it real in your life. A lot of people don't want to get to this point because they want to keep control (which they don't really have) over their lives. As a Christian, you give up your life to get true life and freedom. It doesn't necessarily make any sense to the worldview of things.

And you shall know the truth, and the truth shall make you free…Therefore if the Son makes you free, you shall be free indeed.
- John 8:32 and 36

There is no other freedom on earth like the freedom that Jesus Christ offers and gives to humanity. Some people say that's not freedom because they have to follow all of those rules. It's not about the rules; it's about the relationship to Christ who loves you and therefore you come to love Him. When you love someone, you want to please them and make them happy. That's the relationship that we can have with the creator of the universe. It doesn't make any sense to many people because they do not have the Spirit of God within them. Once a person accepts the free gift from Christ, the Holy Spirit comes inside of them and the Bible says they are a new creation. They understand the spiritual things because they are no longer "natural" humans, not having the Holy Spirit living in them. When a person receives the Spirit, the Bible is a different book to the individual. The understanding that then comes from the words on these pages is life-changing in every respect.

Remember that there is much more to life than what we see and feel around us, because we are spiritual beings, created to have a deep and meaningful relationship with the One who created us.

The thread throughout the entire book of the Bible is that we have a problem (sin) and this separates us from the One who made us. But the good news is that He, through His wisdom and love for us, brought a path forward for anyone willing to accept it. His free gift will restore the relationship by coming into our soul with His spirit dwelling in us and carrying us into eternity with Him. Oh, what a story! If you hear that calling, won't you answer?

No one can come to Me unless the Father who sent Me draws him; and I will raise him up at the last day.
\- John 6:44

CONCLUSION

I want to remind you that it is important to remember that in all of this information, you have to take it in steps. Do not try to comprehend it all at one time. It will overwhelm you and make you not want to even consider all of the pieces to it. So be patient, take it slow, and open your heart. I know that practicing these traits is hard for me to do, too.

In step one we tried to establish the truth and authenticity of the word of God, and that we have more clear evidence of its truth and where it came from and how it eventually got to us. The Bible has been verified and proven as the most consistent document ever compiled by humans. The manuscripts of over forty different writers of the 66 books of the Bible, written over a period of around 1,500 years, in three different languages was preserved for us and it all fits together historically, scientifically and supernaturally.

We then looked in step two at all of the individual books that are in the Bible, and gave just a piece of information out of each one. For thousands of years many people have examined the Bible in order to discredit it, with magnifying glasses looking for problems, errors or contradictions, and then come to the realization that it contains none of these issues. The Bible's truth and power can be verified as well by the evidence of changed history and human lives. The Bible is offered to humankind freely just as the gift of eternal life is offered through Christ. We have our own free will to decide for ourselves the truth of this book or not.

Then finally in step three, we zoomed out from the stories revealed in the Bible to take a look at some of the main ideas or truths. The main reason God created us was His desire to have a relationship with us. But He also knew (HE is omniscient) that we would from the beginning disobey or sin. Even after knowing what we would do, in His plan and purpose, He would come to earth and be born as a human being in Christ. The perfect sinless sacrifice would be the only way for humanity for that relationship with God to be restored. The one major theme revealed throughout the Bible is God's plan of salvation to the entire world by the life, death, and resurrection of Jesus Christ.

The Bible records Jesus saying to people "follow me" or in other words, they were asked to take a step. He came to His disciples in the same manner, never begging them. He just told them to follow Him, to come with Him, to take those steps. He never forced anyone to do anything, as they were always given a choice at what to do. Take a step and open your heart and find the path ahead.

On one occasion the disciples were in a boat and Jesus told them to go on across the lake, and He went to a place by Himself to pray. Later, as they were attempting to go towards the other side while they were on the water, a major storm came about and they all became afraid and thought they were going to die. They looked out and saw Jesus walking on the water coming toward them. At first, they thought they had seen a ghost. They couldn't believe that He was out there walking on the water in the middle of the storm. Peter called out and said to Him, "Lord if it's really you, tell me to come to you on the water." Jesus called out for him to step out of the boat. Peter was the only one willing to take that step as he immediately jumped out of the boat into the water, and began walking on the water himself toward Christ. As he was walking, Peter took his eyes off of Jesus and he began to sink, and the storms became real with the water and waves crashing around. He thought he couldn't really be walking on water! He began to sink because he had taken his eyes off the One who he was believing in. The lesson in this, as we take steps towards God, is that if we keep our eyes on Him and not on the storms that confuse us, He will direct our paths.

Our approach to many things is that we are willing to learn and to take steps towards educating ourselves and finding out about them. But the one thing that we seem hesitant to seek is the truth of our creator. That seems to come harder for us to reach in and see what lies ahead. Why is it so hard for us to want or desire to learn about where we came from, where we are, and where we're going? After all, there are many religions to choose from, so regardless of what people choose it doesn't matter because they can believe whatever they want to believe so you can believe one, all, or none…not really.

When people look at where they buy a car or a new washer and dryer sometimes they really do their homework. I have a friend that will spend months researching, getting all the facts on a new appliance before making the purchase. And you wonder why people aren't willing to do the same research on eternity. Since there are many options, I encourage people to check them out, do some research and find out where their so-called truth came from, and then make up your mind. If you look at Christianity and the Bible strictly from a practical standpoint, you will find the evidence for reliability and accuracy is unmatched with anything else on the planet. The other important fact is the working of the Spirit of God working within a person willing to receive it. This is evidenced by the transforming power in millions of lives around the world.

Often, we just shrug this off and go on like it's not really that important. The truth is, it's the most important thing you'll ever consider in your life. Your soul's destination in eternity depends on it. The journey begins with this as the first step in the rest of your life. Anyone, regardless of their current position in life, can take a few simple steps toward God and unlock indescribable possibilities for the rest of your life.

As a closing statement regarding this book I would like to say that if you take everything away that I have covered, I still know in my heart that the power of Christ is real in my life without any doubt. The two words that I will say is "it's real." Take a step and see for yourself the realness of the power available to you from God in your life by knowing Him. Take a step--you won't regret it!

You have nothing to lose, but you have everything to gain.

"It is in the middle that human choices are made; the beginning and the end remain with God. The decrees of God are birth and death, and in between those limits man makes his own distress or joy." [9]

Romans 10:9,10: that if you confess with your mouth the Lord Jesus and believe in your heart that God has raised Him from the dead, you will be saved. For with the heart one believes unto righteousness, and with the mouth confession is made unto salvation.

BIBLIOGRAPHY

[1] Taken from My Utmost for His Highest, © 1992 by Oswald Chambers. Publications Association, Ltd. Original edition © 1935 by Dodd, Mead & Company, Inc. Copyright renewed 1963 by Oswald Chambers Publications Association, Ltd. All rights reserved.

[2] Taken from The Complete Works of Oswald Chambers © 2000 by Oswald Chambers Publications Association Ltd. Used by permission of Our Daily Bread Publishing. All rights reserved.

[3] Ibid

[4] Ibid

[5] Ibid

[6] Ibid

[7] Ibid

[8] Ibid

[9] Ibid

LOOK FOR
GLEN L. BOLLINGER'S
NEWEST BOOK TO BE
RELEASED BY THE
END OF 2024!

THREE STEPS
WITH GOD

www.ingramcontent.com/pod-product-compliance
Lightning Source LLC
Chambersburg PA
CBHW060516130626
46553CB00002B/518